Ecumenism Means You, Too

Ecumenism Means You, Too

*Ordinary Christians and the Quest
for Christian Unity*

STEVEN R. HARMON

CASCADE *Books* · Eugene, Oregon

ECUMENISM MEANS YOU, TOO
Ordinary Christians and the Quest for Christian Unity

Scripture taken from *The Message*. Copyright © 1993, 1994, 1995,
1996, 2000, 2001, 2002. Used by permission of NavPress Publishing
Group.

Cascade Books
An Imprint of Wipf and Stock Publishers
199 W. 8th Ave., Suite 3
Eugene, OR 97401

www.wipfandstock.com

ISBN 13: 978-1-60608-865-4

Cataloging-in-Publication data:

Harmon, Steven R.

Ecumenism means you, too : ordinary Christians and the quest
for Christian unity / Steven R. Harmon.

xii + 120 p. ; 23 cm.

ISBN 13: 978-1-60608-865-4

1. Church — Catholicity. 2. Ecumenical movement. 3. Church —
Unity. 4. U2 (Musical group). I. Title.

BX1785 .H37 2010

Manufactured in the U.S.A.

For Timothy

*I am grateful to God . . . when I remember you
constantly in my prayers night and day.*
—2 Timothy 1:3 NRSV

Contents

Acknowledgments • *ix*

1 Here to Play Jesus: Why Ecumenism Isn't Dead • 1

2 One, But Not the Same: Ecumenism 101 • 17

3 One Life with Each Other: The Theology of Ecumenism • 39

4 Leaves You If You Don't Care for It: 10 Things You Can Do for the Unity of the Church • 55

5 Hear Us Call: The Eschatology of Ecumenism • 71

Appendix A: Resources for Ecumenical Engagement • *87*

Appendix B: Glossary of Key Ecumenical Terms • *110*

Acknowledgments

THIS BOOK IS A revision and expansion of a series of lectures on the theme "Ecumenism Re-emerging: Christian Young Adults and the Quest for Christian Unity," which I presented as the invited lecturer for the Staley Distinguished Christian Scholar Program at Campbell University in Buies Creek, North Carolina, March 24–26, 2008. I wish to thank the trustees of the Thomas F. Staley Foundation of Larchmont, New York, for providing funding for this program that annually brings distinguished Christian lecturers to Campbell University and numerous other colleges and universities in the United States and Canada. I am grateful also to the members of the administration and faculty of Campbell University responsible for issuing the gracious invitation to deliver these lectures, in particular Jerry M. Wallace, President; M. Dwaine Greene, Provost and Vice President for Academic Affairs; and the members of the lecture series committee that coordinated the Staley Lectures with lectureships sponsored by the Campbell University Divinity School and Department of Religion and Philosophy: Faithe Beam, Campus Minister; Michael G. Cogdill, Dean of the Divinity School; Barry A. Jones, Associate Dean of the Divinity School; W. Glenn Jonas Jr., Chair of the Department of Religion and Philosophy; and Lydia H. Hoyle, Associate Professor of Church History and Baptist Heritage. To be invited to deliver these lectures by the institution that shaped me into the ecumenical theologian I have become was one of the greatest honors ever bestowed on me.

An earlier version of chapter 5 was presented to the Campbell University Baptist Student Union as "U2 and the Eschatology of Ecumenism" on April 3, 2008. Adaptations of chapter 4 have been presented as a workshop session for Beeson Pastors School, Beeson Divinity School, Samford University, Birmingham, Alabama, July 22–25, 2008, and as a workshop session for the General Assembly of the Cooperative Baptist Fellowship, Houston, Texas, July 1–3, 2009. The perceptive questions and comments of those who participated in these sessions have helped me clarify my own thinking about the quest to embody the unity of the church.

Thanks are also due to the members of a course on Theology and the Quest for Christian Unity that I taught at Campbell University Divinity School in the Summer 2007 term: Linda Branscome, Scott Fitzgerald, Rebecca Frederick, Cliff Hobbs, Lisa Koch, Bill Peery, Viveca Pankey, Mark Powell, Laura Reich, Luis Rivas, Lance Rogerson, Joshua Trahan, David Wilson, and Ramona Worsley. Much of the content of this book was hammered out aloud in dialogue with these students that summer, and I am grateful for the way they shaped my thinking about these matters through their thoughtful insights, stimulating questions, and insistence that we keep returning to the practical question of what all of this means for how they will do ministry in local church settings.

This book owes its publication in part to my friend Derek K. Hogan, Theological Reference Librarian and Assistant Professor of New Testament at Campbell University Divinity School. It was Derek who first suggested that

I should consider publishing my Staley Lectures in some form, and I am thankful for the support and encouragement he has long lent to my writing projects.

Dean Timothy F. George and Associate Dean Paul R. House of Samford University's Beeson Divinity School have fostered an institutional climate conducive to productivity in writing for publication that made it possible to prepare this book in the midst of several other research projects and teaching responsibilities. My graduate assistant Robbie Crouse proofread the manuscript with a keen eye and made numerous suggestions for rewording that I trust have helped me communicate more effectively to the readers of this book.

The quotations from *The Message* (Copyright © 1993, 1994, 1995, 1996, 2000, 2001, 2002) that preface each chapter are used by permission of NavPress Publishing Group. *The Message* is a version favored both by Bono and by many among the "ordinary Christians" I hope will read this book, hence its use for this purpose. All other biblical quotations in the text of this book are from the New Revised Standard Version Bible (copyright 1989, Division of Christian Education of the National Council of the Churches of Christ in the United States of America) and are also used by permission. The brief quoted excerpts from the music and lyrics of U2 are published by Blue Mountain Music Ltd (for the UK), Mother Music Ltd (for the Republic Of Ireland), PolyGram International Music, Publishing BV (for The Rest Of The World), and U2 Recordings owned by Universal International Music B.V. exclusively licensed to Island Records (ROW) and Interscope Records (USA).

This book is dedicated to my son Timothy, whose third birthday on May 31, 2009, coincided with Pentecost Sunday and the final few days devoted to this book's preparation for publication (and who has already declared, "Timothy is a U2 fan!"). The dedication of this book to Timothy is especially appropriate, for he spent portions of his first few days in our household strapped to my chest in a carrying sling while I read documents from the Second Vatican Council and typed away at the manuscript for a paper presentation for a bilateral dialogue between the Baptist World Alliance and the Pontifical Council for Promoting Christian Unity. Ecumenism and Timothy have been inextricably linked for me ever since. It is my prayer that he will embody the meaning of his name and "honor God" by one day taking up this book's invitation to seek, in his own way, the unity of the church that is the gift of the one Spirit of Pentecost. My work as an ecumenical theologian has meant that Timothy and my wife Kheresa have had to bear the brunt of my occasional time away from home for participation in ecumenical conferences, not to mention the disruption of a professional relocation during the time this book took shape. I am grateful to them beyond words for the experience of their love in the "church in miniature" that is our family.

Birmingham, Alabama
Pentecost 2009

Here to Play Jesus

Why Ecumenism Isn't Dead

Holy Father, guard them as they pursue this life
That you conferred as a gift through me,
So they can be one heart and mind
As we are one heart and mind.
As long as I was with them, I guarded them
In the pursuit of the life you gave through me;
I even posted a night watch.
And not one of them got away,
Except for the rebel bent on destruction
(the exception that proved the rule of Scripture).

Now I'm returning to you.
I'm saying these things in the world's hearing
So my people can experience
My joy completed in them.
I gave them your word;
The godless world hated them because of it,
Because they didn't join the world's ways,
Just as I didn't join the world's ways.
I'm not asking that you take them out of the world
But that you guard them from the Evil One.
They are no more defined by the world
Than I am defined by the world.

Make them holy—consecrated—with the truth;
Your word is consecrating truth.
In the same way that you gave me a mission in the world,
I give them a mission in the world.
I'm consecrating myself for their sakes
So they'll be truth-consecrated in their mission.

I'm praying not only for them
But also for those who will believe in me
Because of them and their witness about me.
The goal is for all of them to become one heart and mind—
Just as you, Father, are in me and I in you,
So they might be one heart and mind with us.
Then the world might believe that you, in fact, sent me.
The same glory you gave me, I gave them,
So they'll be as unified and together as we are—
I in them and you in me.
Then they'll be mature in this oneness,
And give the godless world evidence
That you've sent me and loved them
In the same way you've loved me.

—John 17:11–23, *The Message*

A COUPLE OF YEARS ago I e-mailed my associate dean at
Campbell University Divinity School to propose teaching a divinity school summer-term course on ecumenism, which is theologian-speak for the quest for Christian unity. His reply kindly commended the proposed course and concluded with the observation, "After all, as U2 said, 'We're one, but we're not the same.'" That line from the band's song "One" (*Achtung Baby*, 1991) was appropriate for that course proposal and this book in more ways than he may have had in mind. Bono has offered various explanations of the song's meaning. It's about a lovers' quarrel; it's about the differences between men and women that pull them together and drive

them apart; it's about a son coming home to tell his father that he's dying of AIDS. Bono lends the song yet another layer of meaning in the band's official memoir *U2 by U2*, where he recounts the pre-history of that line:

> We had a request from the Dalai Lama to participate in a festival called *Oneness*. I love and respect the Dalai Lama but there was something a little bit "let's hold hands hippie" about this particular event. ... I sent him back a note saying, "One—but not the same."[1]

ECUMENISM NOT PLURALISM

Bono's reply to the Dalai Lama's invitation points to an important distinction: ecumenism is not pluralism. Ecumenism is the quest for unity among Christians now divided by denomination. It is not the effort to find some generic essence of religion that might minimize conflicts between the religions. Interreligious dialogue that respects the real differences between the religions is necessary to clear up misunderstandings that Christians, Jews, Muslims, and adherents of other religions may have of one another, and this too is an important task for the church's theologians. But even though interreligious dialogue is sometimes called a "wider ecumenism," it is not the same thing as the quest to embody the unity of the church as the one body of Christ.

Ecumenism is not a relativistic pan-religious pluralism, and the healthiest approaches to ecumenism—the quest for specifically Christian unity—do not minimize the significant differences of faith and practice that exist between churches.

1. Bono, The Edge, Adam Clayton, and Larry Mullen Jr., *U2 by U2* (London: HarperCollins, 2006) 221.

We are one body of Christ, but we are not the same, and it remains to be seen which of our differences are healthy forms of Christian diversity and which differences reflect patterns of faith and practice that must be transformed en route to the full visible unity of the body of Christ.

HOPE FOR THE ECUMENICAL FUTURE

Many observers of the quest for Christian unity are convinced that for a variety of reasons the modern ecumenical movement is dying or already dead. Not everyone is ready to declare this movement dead. One theologian respected internationally as a key long-term participant in the quest for Christian unity has been overheard to remark, "the ecumenical movement isn't dead, but it hasn't breathed in a long time." That may be true. Yet I am hopeful that the ecumenical movement may not only breathe again but even flourish in the future, for many Christians today have perspectives on the church that can contribute to the re-emergence of ecumenism as a vital force in contemporary Christianity.

Typical American Christians increasingly do not feel bound to the denomination of their upbringing. If they were raised in a churchgoing family, they have probably belonged to congregations of more than one denomination along the way. While in college, they routinely attend more than one church, and there's a good chance that those congregations are not of the same denomination. Many younger Christians today are attracted to a tradition significantly different from the one in which they were raised and have experimented with participation in that other tradition. At the Baptist university where I previously taught and delivered the series of lectures that served as the basis of this book, more than a few students came there as Baptists and left as Catholics, Episcopalians, or Presbyterians, for example, and more than a few students came there from another tradition and graduated as Baptists. Some will one day return to embrace the tradition that nurtured them in the faith, while others will continue exploring. At both private and public universities, Christian students' participation in Christian organizations on campus doesn't necessarily match their stated denominational preference. A Baptist Student Union will regularly provide a spiritual home for many non-Baptists. Curious evangelical students may sojourn for awhile with a Roman Catholic-sponsored Newman Center. A great many Christians away for college will eschew the student fellowships sponsored by the denominations of their pre-university nurture for involvement in non-denominational organizations such as InterVarsity Christian Fellowship or Campus Crusade for Christ. These younger Christians tend to attribute denominational divisions to human sinfulness, and they instinctively embrace unity as something that God desires for the body of Christ. Many younger evangelical Christians today have a keen interest in the ancient patterns and practices of worship and spirituality that have continued in the Catholic, Orthodox, and Anglican traditions but have long been absent from evangelicalism. This interest in recovering ancient liturgy for contemporary worship figures prominently in the "emergent" or "emerging church" movement with which many younger Christians identify.[2]

2. Many of these perspectives are described more fully in Robert E. Webber, *The Younger Evangelicals: Facing the Challenges of the New World* (Grand Rapids: Baker, 2002); see especially chapter 7, "Ecclesiology: From Invisible to Visible," 107–23.

Some of these perspectives on the church can also be causes for concern. Abandoning denominational commitments in the interest of being "non-denominational" can actually undermine the quest for Christian unity in some unanticipated ways, and moving easily from a church of one denomination to a congregation of another can be a symptom of the consumer mentality that is endemic to American Christianity. Yet I see aspects of these trends as evidence that a critical mass of ordinary American Christian laypersons want what Christ wants for his church. In the words of the lyric from "One," they know that they are "here to play Jesus."

JESUS'S ECUMENICAL HOPE

The church is indeed "here to play Jesus." While there are limits to this analogy, some theologians build on the biblical image of the church as the "body of Christ" (1 Corinthians 12:27) by speaking of the church as the continuation of the incarnation—the ongoing earthly presence of Christ, the extension of Jesus's earthly ministry in time and space until Jesus comes again.[3] That means that the sorts of things Jesus did and sought during his incarnate life set the agenda for the mission of the church today. Therefore what our Lord wanted then and wants today for his church is what the church should passionately seek. According to chapter 17 of

3. The church as an extension of the incarnation has been a common theme in Catholic theology since J. A. Möhler (d. 1838) and has been taken up by some Eastern Orthodox theologians as well. Jürgen Moltman exemplifies the reservations many Protestant theologians hold regarding this concept in *The Church in the Power of the Spirit: A Contribution to Messianic Ecclesiology*, trans. Margaret Kohl (Philadelphia: Fortress, 1993) 72–73.

the Gospel according to John, on the eve of his crucifixion the main thing Jesus prayed for his followers was "that they may be one" (John 17:11). Four times in the course of this prayer Jesus prays that his disciples and all who later believe through their testimony might have unity: "that they may be one, as we are one" (v. 11); "that they may all be one" (v. 21); "that they may be one, as we are one" (v. 22); "that they may become completely one" (v. 23).

Jesus does ask something else for his followers just before the first prayer for unity. In verse 11 he prays, "Holy Father, protect them." "Protect them"—why? "So that they may be one, as we are one." "Protect them"—from what or from whom? In verse 15 Jesus prays, "I ask you to protect them from the evil one." The "evil one" is the one elsewhere in the New Testament called the "devil," *diabolos* in Greek, which literally means "one who divides." The work of the diabolical one is to bring division, to divide people from God, and to divide people from one another. The evil one seeks especially to bring division to those who ought to have the unity shared by God the Father and God the Son. Thus Jesus prays, "I ask you to protect them from the evil one."

UNITY ACCORDING TO JESUS

The unity Jesus prays for his church is no superficial, "let's hold hands hippie" sort of unity. It is a unity rooted in the life of the one God, who as Father, Son, and Holy Spirit is three distinct persons sharing one divine essence and engaging in one divine work, the redemption of the world. "That they may be one, as we are one," Jesus prays in verses 11 and 22, and in verses 21 and 23 he clarifies these connections: "As you, Father, are in me and I am in you, may they also be in us . . . I in them and you in me."

The ancient Greek theologians had a technical term for the manner in which Jesus's prayer in John 17 portrays the relationships between the persons of the Trinity. The Greek word *perichōrēsis* meant something like "mutual indwelling" or "mutual permeation" or "interpenetration."[4] The eighth-century theologian John of Damascus and others employed this word when they explained the unity of the one God who is three persons, and they cited John 17:23 as the biblical basis of this concept.[5] The being of each person mutually indwells or permeates the being of the other two persons, so that the Father is in the Son and in the Spirit; the Son is in the Spirit and in the Father; and the Spirit is in the Father and in the Son. Each person jointly participates in the work of the other two persons. When the Father creates the heavens and the earth and makes human beings in the image of God and gives them life, the Son and the Spirit jointly share in the divine work of creation. When the Son comes down from heaven and becomes incarnate for us and for our salvation, suffers and dies for our sins on the cross, is raised from the dead, ascends into heaven, sits at the right hand of the Father, and comes again to judge the living and the dead, the Father and the Spirit jointly share in the divine work of redemption. When the Spirit indwells the lives of believers, makes them holy, and empowers the Christian

4. G. W. H. Lampe, *A Patristic Greek Lexicon* (Oxford: Clarendon, 1961) s.v. "*perichōrēsis, hē*."

5. John of Damascus *De Fide Orthodoxa* 1.8 (English translation, "Exposition of the Orthodox Faith," trans. S. D. F. Salmond, in *Nicene and Post-Nicene Fathers*, Second Series [New York: Scriber's, 1899; reprint edition, Peabody, MA: Hendrickson, 1994] vol. 9, 10–11).

life, the Father and the Son jointly share in the divine work of sustaining what God has created and redeemed. This understanding of Trinitarian *perichōrēsis* is the concept behind the familiar Trinitarian symbol of three interlocking circles in which each circle is intertwined with and inseparable from the other two.

The source of the church's unity is nothing less than the unifying life of the one God who dwells in us and makes us one. The unity of the shared life and work of the three persons of the Trinity is the model and standard for the unity that ought to characterize the church. Therefore Christian unity is a perichoretic unity. That means that the lives of churches in relationship to other churches and the lives of individual believers in relationship to other believers ought to be as inseparably intertwined as the three interlocking circles that symbolize the Trinity. In other words, we are "members of one another," as Scripture tells us more than once (Rom 12:5, Eph 4:25; cf. also 1 Cor 12:20–26).

The unity for which our Lord prayed is the kind of unity that belongs to the one God who is Father, Son, and Holy Spirit, and it falls short of that unity if it is not a unity the world can see. In verses 21 and 23, the purpose of Christian unity is evangelistic—that is to say, it has as its ultimate end the conversion of the world: "so that the world may believe that you have sent me. . . . so that the world may know that you have sent me and have loved them even as you have loved me." That is why many participants in the ecumenical movement emphasize visible unity as the goal of ecumenism. As the result of our divisions, we are not yet united at the Lord's table. Our churches do not yet all recognize one another's baptisms as the one baptism of the one body of Christ. We are not yet able to speak with one prophetic voice against the world's injustices. Our divisions have compromised our witness so that the world does not find it compelling.

DIVISION AND DISBELIEF

The backstory of the band that sings "One" embodies this connection between a divided church and a disbelieving society. U2 is an Irish band, and the span of their career encompasses some of the bloodiest episodes in the troubles in neighboring Northern Ireland. Their artistic yearning for a place "where the streets have no name" grew out of a holy dissatisfaction with a place where the street where one lived also indicated whether one was Catholic or Protestant, and often whether one's political sympathies were Irish Republican or Ulster Unionist. The religious divide that fractured Irish society also ran right down the middle of the band. Guitarist The Edge and bass player Adam Clayton were from Protestant families; drummer Larry Mullen Jr.'s family was Catholic; and Bono was the offspring of a "mixed marriage"—a Catholic father and Protestant mother. Three members of the band embraced faith in Christ beyond those traditional divisions of Irish Christianity in the Shalom Community, a non-denominational charismatic fellowship. While they later left that church when it became increasingly legalistic, they maintained close relations over the years with several members of that community who had formed them in the faith.

Today all four members of the band are committed Christians—though perhaps not the best examples of active churchmanship. Their seeming distance from the life of the institutional church stems not only from the traumatic local church experience of their youth but more broadly from disillusionment over the church's contributions to the explosive mix of religious factionalism, patriolatry, and violence—"your Sermon on the Mount from the boot of your car," as their song "Please" (*Pop*, 1997) depicts the twisted religious motivation of an IRA car bombing. U2's faith survived, but they bucked the trend: the thirty years of the Northern Ireland conflict paralleled a period of increasing Irish disenchantment with the church, despite the fact that the Republic of Ireland had—and still has—one of the highest official religious identification percentages in the world. Many during that time would have identified with the outlook of Irish rock critic Bill Graham, a self-described "typically Irish ex-Catholic agnostic," who was shocked and initially appalled when Bono announced in an interview with him early in U2's career, "One other thing you should know . . . we're all Christians."[6] When the world cannot see a united church, the world may stand aloof from union with God.

HOPE DESPITE DISCOURAGEMENT

Even in their angry soapbox lament for the troubles, "Sunday Bloody Sunday" (*War*, 1983), U2 doesn't allow present discouragement to dash hopes for an ecumenical future: "Tonight, we can be as one," they sing, if we "claim the victory Jesus won." Today there are plenty of reasons to be discouraged about the future of ecumenism. Like the "broken bottles round the children's feet/bodies strewn across a dead-end street" in "Sunday Bloody Sunday," the tragic evidence of our

6. Bill Graham, *Another Time, Another Place* (London: Mandarin, 1989) 24.

lack of Christian unity can cause us to lose heart and resign ourselves to our continued conflict and division. Despite the amazing accomplishments of the ecumenical movement in the past century, visible unity seems ever more distant. In the opinion of some experienced ecumenists, the institutions of international ecumenism have given less and less attention to their work on the issues of doctrine and church order that must be contested before visible unity can become a reality, and their increasing emphasis on political and so-cial challenges faced by the contemporary church—while understandable and in certain respects even necessary to ecumenical advance—has sometimes contributed to further divisions. The ecumenical leaders of the past few decades are retiring and passing away, and few younger leaders are ready to take up their mantle. The denominations that were once heavily invested in the quest for Christian unity have now turned their energies to their worsening internal divi-sions. Conflicts *within* denominations over biblical author-ity, gender, and sexuality have greatly complicated efforts to secure unity *between* the denominations. Media mischar-acterizations of recent statements by the Vatican on the relation of the Roman Catholic Church to other Christian communities have led to knee-jerk reactions that threaten the progress already made in Protestant-Catholic dialogue.[7]

7. On July 10, 2007, the Vatican released a June 29 document from the Congregation for the Doctrine of the Faith offering "Responses to Some Questions Regarding Certain Aspects of the Doctrine of the Church" (Online: www.vatican.va/roman_curia/congregations/cfaith/documents /rc_con_cfaith_doc_20070629_responsa-quaestiones_en.html). Even though this document clearly reiterated what the Vatican II Decree on Ecumenism *Unitatis Redintegratio* ("The Repair of Unity," 1964) and John Paul II's papal encyclical on Christian unity *Ut Unum Sint* ("That They May Be One," 1995) had generously affirmed regarding the pres-

Convergences attained in international conversations between denominations often have not been well received at the local level, and frequently local church leaders remain unaware of these agreements.[8]

Ecumenical despair is understandable, given the circumstances. But we can yet be as one, because the ecumenical movement is not dead. The quest for Christian unity will breathe again because on Easter Sunday Jesus has already won the victory over the diabolical forces of division. It will breathe again because Christian young adults are here to play Jesus. They instinctively want the unity Jesus wants for his church. I am hopeful about the ecumenical future because I have seen the ecumenical potential of the ordinary Christian laypersons I've known on university campuses and in local churches. I've written this book to encourage them to embrace with intentionality their intuitions about

ence of Christ and the work of the Spirit in other churches and ecclesial communities that are separated from the Roman Catholic Church, media mischaracterizations of the document contributed to worldwide outrage at what many regarded as a major step away from the Rome's post-Vatican II commitments to ecumenical engagement. Chapter 2 of this book will explain more fully the significance of the Second Vatican Council and other developments within Roman Catholicism for the ecumenical movement.

8. Seasoned theological leaders of the ecumenical movement have identified the aforementioned factors as contributors to the movement's current malaise. See William G. Rusch, "The State and Future of the Ecumenical Movement," *Pro Ecclesia* 9:1 (2000) 8–18; Carl E. Braaten and Robert W. Jenson, eds., *In One Body through the Cross: The Princeton Proposal for Christian Unity* (Grand Rapids: Eerdmans, 2003) 6–7; George Lindbeck, "Ecumenisms in Conflict," in *God, Truth, and Witness: Engaging Stanley Hauerwas*, ed. L. Gregory Jones et al. (Grand Rapids: Brazos, 2005) 212–28; Robert W. Jenson, "God's Time, Our Time: An Interview with Robert W. Jenson," *Christian Century* 123:9 (May 2, 2006) 31–35.

the unity of the church. I hope the readers of this book will become the future leaders of a renewed ecumenical movement—especially as laity (and clergy, too) who will embody grassroots ecumenism in local church contexts, but also as those who will invest their lives in seeking the unity of the church as a new generation of denominational leaders and educators.

YOU, TOO, CAN BE AN ECUMENIST

Ecumenism Means You, Too is not a book about theological themes in the music of U2. Now that these themes have persisted across the three-decade span of the band's career, ministers and academic theologians have already written such books.[9] This book rather invokes the theological dimensions of U2 songs when they cast artistic light on various aspects of the quest for Christian unity. The lyrics of "One" and other songs referenced in each chapter do not have the unity of the church in mind, yet the Christian theological framework apart from which the import of U2's art cannot be fully appreciated is the same framework that makes sense of the ecumenical enterprise. The members of the band would probably not agree with my interpretations of that theological framework and how it functions in their music, nor with everything that I have to say about

9. Greg Garrett, *We Get to Carry Each Other: The Gospel According to U2* (Louisville, KY: Westminster John Knox, 2009); Christian Scharen, *One Step Closer: Why U2 Matters to Those Seeking God* (Grand Rapids: Brazos, 2006); Robert Vagacs, *Religious Nuts, Political Fanatics: U2 in Theological Perspective* (Eugene, OR: Cascade, 2005); Steve Stockman, *Walk On: The Spiritual Journey of U2*, rev. ed. (Orlando, FL: Relevant, 2005); Raewynne J. Whiteley and Beth Maynard, eds., *Get Up Off Your Knees: Preaching the U2 Catalog* (Cambridge, MA: Cowley, 2003).

the nature of Christian unity (though I imagine that they might concur that the visible oneness of the body of Christ is a good thing). Nonetheless, U2 and their music will help me make the case that inasmuch as seeking the unity of the body of Christ is an inescapable obligation of Christian discipleship, ecumenism means *you, too* (and I hope you'll pardon the pun).

Toward that end, the chapter titles incorporate snippets from the lyrics of the studio version of "One," plus an extended coda from live concert performances of the song on tour in the case of the final chapter. Chapter 2, "One, but Not the Same: Ecumenism 101," is an introduction to the history of the ecumenical movement and the divisions that it seeks to heal. Chapter 3, "One Life with Each Other: The Theology of Ecumenism," explains the biblically grounded theological concepts that drive the quest for visible unity and make it an unavoidable obligation for all churches and all Christians. Chapter 4, "Leaves You If You Don't Care for It: 10 Things You Can Do for the Unity of the Church," outlines an action plan for ecumenism as an embodied practice of grassroots Christian activism in which all Christians can and must participate. Chapter 5, "Hear Us Call: The Eschatology of Ecumenism," is a theological epilogue that encourages patient perseverance toward a goal that is not likely to be realized in the lifetime of anyone reading this book (but God has done surprising things before, and may yet again in our lifetimes). Appendix 1, "Resources for Ecumenical Engagement," provides an annotated bibliography of books, periodicals, and Internet resources that will provide additional help for those who may take up the challenge of this book to pray and work for the unity of the body of Christ. Appendix 2, "Glossary of Key Ecumenical Terms," defines the technical language that may be encountered when utilizing those resources.

Many of the resources included in Appendix 1 will make concrete proposals for convergence on the issues that continue to divide the church, to which I hope readers will give serious future consideration. In this book I refrain from making any such specific proposals for ecumenical progress, save one: that the quest for Christian unity includes *you, too*, and its future depends in part on your personal commitment to embark on that quest as a matter of being a faithful follower of Jesus Christ.

2

One, But Not the Same

Ecumenism 101

I have a serious concern to bring up with you, my friends, using the authority of Jesus, our Master. I'll put it as urgently as I can: You must get along with each other. You must learn to be considerate of one another, cultivating a life in common. I bring this up because some from Chloe's family brought a most disturbing report to my attention—that you're fighting among yourselves! I'll tell you exactly what I was told: You're all picking sides, going around saying, "I'm on Paul's side," or "I'm for Apollos," or "Peter is my man," or "I'm in the Messiah group." I ask you, "Has the Messiah been chopped up in little pieces so we can each have a relic all our own? Was Paul crucified for you? Was a single one of you baptized in Paul's name?"

—1 Corinthians 1:10–13, *The Message*

Regarding this next item, I'm not at all pleased. I am getting the picture that when you meet together it brings out your worst side instead of your best! First, I get this report on your divisiveness, competing with and criticizing each other. I'm reluctant to believe it, but there it is. The best that can be said for

it is that the testing process will bring truth into the
open and confirm it.

—1 Corinthians 11:17–19, *The Message*

THE PROPER STARTING POINT for this chapter is not the
"One" lyric quoted in its title, but another line from
the same song: "We hurt each other, and we do it again." To
speak of a quest for Christian unity is to imply its current
lack. The story of the ecumenical movement is therefore
inseparable from the story of how the church lost its unity.
The latter is a tragic tale of failures in Christian love that
offers countless negative examples of the works of the flesh
rather than the fruit of the Spirit. Yet knowing something
about the story of Christian division helps us speak the
truth in love by reminding us that our disagreements are
not insignificant. Whether we are considering the divisions
that resulted from heretical teachings about the nature of
God and the person of Christ in the first few centuries of the
church, the eleventh-century schism between what we now
call the Roman Catholic and Eastern Orthodox churches,
the countless divisions of the Western church that stem
from the Reformation in the sixteenth century, or the more
recent divisions within denominations that have to do with
divided responses to modernity, many aspects of all of these
divisions have to do with crucial issues of faith and practice.
We contest these things with one another because we seek
a Truth beyond ourselves, and reckoning seriously with the
sources of our divisions makes us ever aware that now we
"know only in part" (1 Cor 13:12). The *Decree on Ecumenism*
from the Second Vatican Council recognizes this benefit of
contesting our divisions when it says, "Thus the way will be
opened by which through fraternal rivalry all will be stirred

to a deeper understanding and a clearer presentation of the unfathomable riches of Christ."[1]

HERESY AND THE REPAIR OF UNITY

The modern ecumenical movement began in earnest early in the twentieth century, but there have been organized attempts to recover the visible unity of the church as long as there have been divisions in the church—which means the quest for Christian unity has been going on for two millennia. The first efforts at ecumenism were responses to threats to the integrity of the church posed by early Christian heresies.

Many American Christians have an acute allergic reaction to the suggestion that something should be regarded as heresy by the church. Because we have absorbed the relativism of our culture, we tend to consider it unacceptable to find another's faith unacceptable. A heretic, however, is not merely someone who holds ideas that the powers that be in the church consider wrongheaded. It's not quite that easy to be a heretic. In 1 Cor 11:18–19 the Apostle Paul addresses the "divisions" that have occurred in the church at Corinth. In verse 19 he uses the Greek word *hairēseis*, which in transliteration supplies our English word "heresies," as a near synonym for the "divisions" mentioned in verse 18 (Greek *schismata*, the source of the English word "schisms"). The nearly identical meaning of the two words is reflected in the translation of *schismata* in verse 18 as "divisions" and *hairēseis* in verse 19 as "factions" in several English

1. Vatican II, "Decree on Ecumenism" (*Unitatis redintegratio*) November 21, 1964. Online: www.vatican.va/archive/hist_councils/ ii_vatican_council/documents/vat-ii_decree_19641121_unitatis- redintegratio_en.html.

versions, but there is also a shade of difference in meaning so that *hairēseis* qualifies the nature of the *schismata*. The Corinthian divisions resulted in part from heresies, which are self-chosen opinions that divide the church when they are introduced into the teaching that takes place within it.[2]

In light of Paul's use of the Greek word for "heresies" in this passage and in light of the nature of early heresies in the first few centuries of the church, it seems that one has to fulfill three criteria in order to be a heretic in the fullest classical sense of the word.

First, a heretic is someone whose account of the Christian story is so dangerously inadequate that it's really an altogether different story than the biblical story of the Triune God. One such radically different telling of the Christian story was Gnosticism (from the Greek word *gnōsis*, "knowledge"). The second-century Gnostics claimed a secret insight into the true nature of Christianity that was really rooted in a Platonic dualism between the good realm of spirit/idea and the evil realm of matter/flesh. Gnosticism met this criterion of heresy because according to its version of the divine story, God could not have anything to do with an essentially evil material order and humanity could be saved only by escaping it. Arianism was a fourth-century heresy that maintained that the Son's divinity was of a different and lesser order than the Father's divinity. The teachings of Arius (d. 336) and his followers also met this criterion be-

---

2. These contextual connotations of Paul's use of this language in 1 Cor 11:18–19 are reinforced by the interrelationship between the semantic domains of *hairesis* in early Christian usage ("choice," "opinion," and "division") in Heinrich Schlier's entry *"haireomai, hairēsis"* in *Theological Dictionary of the New Testament*, ed. Gerhard Kittel, trans. Geoffrey W. Bromiley (Grand Rapids: Eerdmans, 1964) 1:180–85.

cause they too distanced the fullness of God from the work of redeeming humanity through the incarnation, delegating the work of salvation to that which is less than the fullness of God.

Second, one must also teach this alternative version of the Christian story as an authoritative teacher in the church—or at least as someone who wants to be recognized as a teacher. Many people entertain ideas that would be heretical if they were taught, but not everyone teaches them.

Third, to be a heretic one must insist that this dangerously inadequate telling of the Christian story be regarded by the church as acceptable teaching and through this insistence threaten to divide the church. Heresy is therefore not only about problematic theological ideas. It also involves divisive behavior toward the church. Heresy is therefore as much a matter of ethics as it is of doctrine.

CONTESTING THE FAITH AS A STEP TOWARD UNITY

After the emperor Constantine (d. 337) ended imperially endorsed persecution of the church early in the fourth century, the church began responding to heresies by convening ecumenical councils. These church councils were "ecumenical" in two senses of the word. They were ecumenical in that they involved representatives from the whole of the inhabited Christian world. This is the original sense of the Greek word *oikoumenē* from which we get our words "ecumenical" and "ecumenism." They were also ecumenical in that their aim was not to divide the church into heretics and non-heretics but rather to unite the church by clarifying the church's faith and practice. They passionately contested the issues at stake so that all parties in the debates might come to a more complete understanding of the truth. From 325 to 787 CE, bishops from all over the Christian world met in seven ecumenical councils. They sought greater unity on issues that were vital to the integrity of the faith and its relevance to the world.

The First Council of Nicaea (325) and the First Council of Constantinople (381) clarified the relationship of Christ the Son and the Holy Spirit to the divinity of God the Father and the significance of that relationship for the salvation of humanity—in other words, the doctrine of the Trinity and why it matters. The Council of Ephesus (431), the Council of Chalcedon (451), the Second Council of Constantinople (553), and the Third Council of Constantinople (680–81) each addressed different dimensions of two interrelated questions: How are the divine and human natures of Jesus Christ related to one another in the one person of the incarnation of God the Son? And what does the union of divinity and humanity in Jesus Christ mean for the experience of salvation and the living of the Christian life? The Second Council of Nicaea (787) sought to resolve controversies over the veneration (a term that means "reverence," not worship) of icons. The issues at stake in the Seventh Ecumenical Council, and especially its ultimate affirmation of the veneration of icons, may seem alien to many evangelical Christians today. But the iconoclastic controversy and its resolution at Nicaea II were more broadly concerned with the implications of God's relation to the material order in the incarnation for the role of the material order in Christian worship, something that ought to concern all Christians.

The main subjects debated by the ecumenical councils were hardly trivial concerns. It would have been disastrous for the future of Christianity if the factions divided over doctrine had simply agreed to disagree. The outcome of some of these councils did result in continued division. But had the ecumenical councils decided differently, they would have rendered Christianity irrelevant. We would have been left with a gospel that is no good news at all, for the alternative to the decisions of the ecumenical councils would be the story of a God who stands distant from us, who does not participate personally in our salvation—if indeed such a God could save us at all—and to whom our materiality doesn't matter, as well as a Christ who cannot be followed. Ecumenism at its best is in continuity with this aspect of the ecumenism of the ecumenical councils. It seeks unity in the truth, and not a unity that comes at the expense of the truth.

THE CHURCH BREATHING WITH BOTH LUNGS

In 1054 a schism between the Eastern and Western churches over long-standing differences in theology, liturgy, politics, language, and culture divided the church geographically in half. Yet in the aftermath of this schism neither Constantinople nor Rome wanted the division to continue indefinitely. Reunion councils were held in Lyons in 1274 and Florence in 1439, and representatives of the Roman Catholic and Eastern Orthodox churches did reach agreement on some of the theological issues contested by them in these councils. But when they returned home, the agreements fell apart for reasons largely political, and the churches remained divided.

Since the Second Vatican Council, however, relations between Roman Catholicism and the Orthodox churches have made dramatic steps forward. In 1965, Pope Paul VI (1897–1978) and Patriarch of Constantinople Athenagoras I (1886–1972) issued a joint declaration that withdrew the mutual excommunications and condemnations of 1054.[3] Pope John Paul II (1920–2005) frequently voiced his hope that one day the church might be able to "breathe with both her lungs," East and West, and today the two churches are closer to full visible unity with each other than they are with any other Christian churches. The *Catechism of the Catholic Church* teaches, "With the Orthodox Churches, this communion is so profound that it lacks little to attain the fullness that would permit a common celebration of the Lord's Eucharist."[4]

REFORMING THE ONE, HOLY, CATHOLIC, AND APOSTOLIC CHURCH

The early Protestant Reformers of the sixteenth century likewise did not want their separation from the Roman Church to be permanent. They understood themselves not as separatists but as a reforming movement within the one, holy, catholic, and apostolic church (the four classical "marks of the church" from the Nicene Creed, which the Reformers also embraced). Martin Luther (1483–1546) had no wish to start a new church. He did offer an uncompromising prophetic critique of his own Roman Catholic Church concern-

3. Paul VI and Athenagoras I, "Joint Catholic-Orthodox Declaration of His Holiness Pope Paul VI and the Ecumenical Patriarch Athenagoras I," December 7, 1965. Online: www.vatican.va/holy_father/paul_vi/speeches/1965/documents/hf_p-vi_spe_19651207_common-declaration_en.html.

4. *Catechism of the Catholic Church* (Liguori, MO: Liguori, 1994) § 838 (p. 222).

ing developments that he believed jeopardized the integrity of the gospel, and he regarded the resulting divisions as temporarily necessary but ultimately inconsistent with Christ's will for his church. This first division of the Reformation was not an intentional separation with the goal of establishing or restoring a true church, but rather an unintended tragedy occasioned by a complex set of social, political, ecclesiastical, and historical circumstances.[5]

John Calvin (1509–1564), the greatest systematic theologian among the early Reformers, was also arguably the movement's first major ecumenist.[6] He personally attended theological dialogues between Roman Catholics and Lutherans, and he longed for a general council of the European evangelical churches that might unify the rapidly multiplying divisions in the churches of the Protestant Reformation. Such a council never came to pass, but Calvin's ecumenical passion is reflected in a couple of quotations addressed to other Christian leaders of that time. To the Anglican Archbishop of Canterbury Thomas Cranmer (1489–1556) he wrote:

> This other thing also is to be ranked among the chief evils of our time, viz., that the Churches are so divided that human fellowship is scarcely now of any repute among us, far less that Christian intercourse which all profess but few sincerely practice. ... [T]he very heaviest blame attaches to the leaders themselves who, either engrossed in their own sin-

5. This reading of Luther's stance toward the Catholic Church is exemplified by David S. Yeago, "The Catholic Luther," in *The Catholicity of the Reformation*, ed. Carl E. Braaten and Robert W. Jenson (Grand Rapids: Eerdmans, 1996) 13–34.

6. John T. McNeill, "Calvin as an Ecumenical Churchman," *Church History* 32 (December 1963) 379–91.

ful pursuits, are indifferent to the safety and entire piety of the Church, or who, individually satisfied with their own private peace, have no regard for others. Thus it is that the members of the Church being severed, the body lies bleeding. So much does this concern me that, could I be of any service, I would not grudge to cross even ten seas, if need were, on account of it. . . . I think it right for me, at whatever cost of toil and trouble, to seek to obtain this object.[7]

Calvin's hope for a more visibly unified church was not limited to the divided churches of the Reformation. He also wrote this in reply to the Roman Catholic cardinal James Sadoleto (1477–1547), who had written a letter to the leaders and people of Geneva that pleaded with them to return to communion with the Church of Rome:

The Lord grant, Sadoleto, that you and all your party may at length perceive that the only true bond of ecclesiastical unity consists in this, that Christ the Lord, who has reconciled us to God the Father, gather us out of our present dispersion into the fellowship of his body, that so, through his one Word and Spirit, we may join together with one heart and one soul.[8]

Calvin did not shrink from naming the serious disagreements that precluded an easy return to unity with Rome, but he also did not abandon the hope that the gracious work

7. John Calvin to Thomas Cranmer, April 1552, in *Letters of John Calvin*, ed. and trans. Jules Bonnet (New York: Burt Franklin, 1858) vol. 2, 347–48.

8. John Calvin to James Cardinal Sadoleto, September 1, 1539, in *Calvin: Theological Treatises*, ed. and trans. J. K. S. Reid. Library of Christian Classics (Philadelphia: Westminster, 1954) vol. 23, 256.

of the Triune God might yet gather the Church of Rome and the churches of the Reformation into one united church.

The early Reformation confessions were ecumenical in their intent. They were drafted at first to explain the Reformers' positions so that they might find unity within the Roman church, and then to seek unity among the churches of the Reformation. The Reformers would have been shocked and grieved by our easy acceptance of the divisions of the church today.

UNITY AND MISSION

It is no mere historical accident that the beginnings of the modern ecumenical movement in the nineteenth century coincided with the beginnings of the modern missions movement. The missionaries quickly concluded that taking a divided Christianity to the mission field harmed their witness for Christ, and some of them issued the earliest modern calls for ecumenical convergence. In 1806, William Carey (1761–1834), a Baptist missionary to India, proposed that "a general association of all denominations of Christians from the four quarters of the earth" meet each decade at the Cape of Good Hope.[9] Carey's dream was realized in part by the World Missionary Conference held in Edinburgh, Scotland, in 1910 that led to the founding of the ongoing International Missionary Conference in 1921. While these gatherings were initially limited to Protestants, they served as the nucleus for what became the primary institutional expression of the worldwide ecumenical movement.

9. William Carey to Andrew Fuller, Calcutta, May 15, 1806; quoted in Timothy F. George, *Faithful Witness: The Life and Mission of William Carey* (Birmingham: New Hope, 1991) 163.

One of the speakers at the Edinburgh World Missionary Conference was an Episcopal missionary to the Philippines from the United States, Bishop Charles Brent (1862–1929). Bishop Brent urged conference participants not to be content with merely seeking greater cooperation in missions among the denominations, for visible unity would require that divisive issues of doctrine and church order be addressed. He called for the creation of an international commission devoted to the ecumenical study of the matters of faith and order that presently divided the churches, and he personally made this proposal to representatives of the Roman Catholic Church, the Eastern Orthodox churches, and the various Protestant communions.[10] In 1927, a World Conference on Faith and Order held its initial meeting in Lausanne, Switzerland, with representatives of all major Christian communions, including the Orthodox, but with the exception of the Roman Catholic Church. Two years earlier, the Conference on Life and Work had been founded in Stockholm, Sweden, to seek worldwide cooperation between the churches in addressing social issues. A young Dietrich Bonhoeffer (1906–1945), whose books *The Cost of Discipleship*, *Letters and Papers from Prison*, and *Life Together* are now regarded as devotional classics, was one of the early participants in the Life and Work movement.[11]

10. Alexander C. Zabriskie, *Bishop Brent, Crusader for Christian Unity* (Philadelphia: Westminster, 1948).

11. Eberhard Bethge, *Dietrich Bonhoeffer: Man of Vision, Man of Courage*, trans. Eric Mosbacher and others (New York: Harper & Row, 1970) 146–53.

THE INSTITUTIONAL FACE
OF INTERNATIONAL ECUMENISM

These three complementary expressions of the worldwide ecumenical movement—cooperation in mission, joint exploration of doctrine and church order, and solidarity in social action—ultimately coalesced in a unified institutional embodiment of the quest for Christian unity. In 1948 the Life and Work and Faith and Order movements joined to form the World Council of Churches, and in 1961 the International Missionary Conference also merged into the WCC. The ecumenical movement has been its healthiest when these three emphases—mission, doctrine, and social justice—have gone hand in hand. It has suffered whenever any one of those emphases has dominated to the neglect of the others.

The Third Assembly of the World Council of Churches in New Delhi, India, in 1961 also issued what is now regarded as the classic definition of the visible unity sought by the ecumenical movement. Drafted by Methodist theologian Albert Outler (1908–1989), the statement reads:

> We believe that the unity which is both God's will and his gift to his Church is being made visible as all in each place who are baptized into Jesus Christ and confess him as Lord and Savior are brought by the Holy Spirit into one fully-committed fellowship, holding the one apostolic faith, preaching the one Gospel, breaking the one bread, joining in common prayer, and having a corporate life reaching out in witness and service to all and who at the same time are united with the whole Christian fellowship in all places and all ages, in such wise that ministry and members are accepted by all, and that all can

> act and speak together as occasion requires for the
> tasks to which God calls his people.[12]

The New Delhi definition is now commonly embraced as
the best concise explanation of the goal of the ecumenical
movement: a visible unity in which all baptized Christians—
in every place there are Christians—fully belong to one
another in a covenanted community that is both local and
worldwide in which they share the historic faith of the
church, are able to share in the celebration of the Eucharist
together, jointly engage in mission and service, accept the
ministers and members of one another's churches as their
own, and speak prophetic words to the world with a unified
voice whenever God calls them to do so.

VATICAN II AND ROMAN CATHOLIC ECUMENISM

We're still a long way from the sort of visible unity envisioned
by the New Delhi definition. But it became a less unrealistic
hope when the Roman Catholic Church officially embraced
the worldwide ecumenical movement at the Second Vatican
Council that convened from 1962 to 1965. In preparation
for the Council, the Vatican established a Secretariat for
Promoting Christian Unity and extended invitations to
other churches and denominations to send official observers. One of the most significant developments of Vatican II
was the unanimous approval on November 21, 1964, of the
Decree on Ecumenism *Unitatis Redintegratio* quoted earlier
in this chapter. After acknowledging that "division openly

12. "Report of the Section on Unity," in *The New Delhi Report: The
Third Assembly of the World Council of Churches, 1961* (New York:
Association, 1962) 116.

contradicts the will of Christ, scandalizes the world, and damages the holy cause of preaching the Gospel to every creature," the decree recognizes the modern ecumenical movement that began among Protestants as nothing less than the work of God:

> In recent times more than ever before, He has been rousing divided Christians to remorse over their divisions and to a longing for unity. Everywhere large numbers have felt the impulse of this grace, and among our separated brethren also there increases from day to day the movement, fostered by the grace of the Holy Spirit, for the restoration of unity among all Christians. . . . [A]lmost everyone regards the body in which he has heard the Gospel as his Church and indeed, God's Church. All however, though in different ways, long for the one visible Church of God, a Church truly universal and set forth into the world that the world may be converted to the Gospel and so be saved, to the glory of God.[13]

This *Decree on Ecumenism* was the major twentieth-century turning point in the progress of the quest for Christian unity. It acknowledged that all churches, including the Roman Catholic Church, share responsibility for their contributions to the present divisions. It explicitly affirmed that non-Catholic Christians experience the grace of God through the presence of Christ and the work of the Spirit in Christian communities that are outside the Roman Catholic Church. While mainstream media treatments of

13. Vatican II, "Decree on Ecumenism" (*Unitatis Redintegratio*) November 21, 1964. Online: www.vatican.va/archive/hist_councils/ ii_vatican_council/documents/vat-ii_decree_19641121_unitatis-redintegratio_en.html.

recent Vatican statements on the status of Christian communities outside the Catholic Church have interpreted these statements as movements away from the ecumenical gains of Vatican II, closer examination of their content shows that their intent is otherwise.[14] Pope John Paul II and Pope Benedict XVI (1927–) have in fact re-affirmed what the *Decree on Ecumenism* teaches Roman Catholics about non-Catholic Christians and their churches.[15] The decree called for all Catholics, clergy and laity alike, to learn about and learn from the distinctive gifts that the other denominational traditions contribute to the body of Christ. It irrevocably committed the Roman Catholic Church to participation in the various forms of the worldwide ecumenical movement, and thus it also opened the way for many other denominations to follow through on their own ecumenical convictions by entering into formal dialogue with Roman Catholicism.

14. Congregation for the Doctrine of the Faith, "Declaration '*Dominus Iesus*' on the Unicity and Salvific Universality of Jesus Christ and the Church," August 6, 2000. Online: www.vatican.va/roman_curia/congregations/cfaith/documents/rc_con_cfaith_doc_20000806_dominus-iesus_en.html; and "Responses to Some Questions Regarding Certain Aspects of the Doctrine of the Church," June 29, 2007. Online: www.vatican.va/roman_curia/congregations/cfaith/documents/rc_con_cfaith_doc_20070629_responsa-quaestiones_en.html.

15. John Paul II, "On Commitment to Ecumenism" (*Ut unum sint*) May 25, 1995. Online: www.vatican.va/holy_father/john_paul_ii/encyclicals/documents/hf_jp-ii_enc_25051995_ut-unum-sint_en.html; Benedict XVI, General Audience, Paul VI Audience Hall, January 23, 2008. Online: www.vatican.va/holy_father/benedict_xvi/audiences/2008/documents/hf_ben-xvi_aud_20080123_en.html.

COME, LET US REASON TOGETHER:
ENGAGING IN DIALOGUE

The changed ecumenical situation that followed Vatican II fostered numerous bilateral and multilateral dialogues between representatives of various denominations. Over the past four decades these dialogues have produced a rich body of agreed statements that document strides toward unity in faith and practice along with the matters of continued disagreement that warrant future dialogue.[16] The international communion of my own denomination, the Baptist World Alliance, has engaged in bilateral dialogues with the Lutheran World Federation, the World Alliance of Reformed Churches, the World Mennonite Conference, the Anglican Consultative Council, and the Roman Catholic Pontifical Council for Promoting Christian Unity, and preliminary conversations have been held with the Orthodox Ecumenical Patriarchate.[17] The most exciting outcome

16. See "The Nature, Goal, and Reception of Dialogues," chap. 6 in *Introduction to Ecumenism* by Jeffrey Gros, Eamon McManus, and Ann Riggs (New York: Paulist, 1998).

17. Baptist World Alliance and World Alliance of Reformed Churches, *Baptists and Reformed in Dialogue: Documents from the Conversations Sponsored by the World Alliance of Reformed Churches and the Baptist World Alliance*, ed. Larry Miller. Studies from the World Alliance of Reformed Churches, no. 4 (Geneva: World Alliance of Reformed Churches, 1983). Online: http://warc.jalb.de/warcajsp/news_file/4.pdf; Baptist World Alliance and Secretariat for Promoting Christian Unity, "Summons to Witness to Christ in Today's World: A Report on the Baptist-Roman Catholic International Conversations, 1984–1988," in *Deepening Communion: International Ecumenical Documents with Roman Catholic Participation*, ed. William G. Rusch and Jeffrey Gros (Washington, DC: United States Catholic Conference, 1998) 343–60. Online: http://www.prounione.urbe.it/dia-int/b-rc/doc/e_b-rc_report1988_01.html; Baptist-Lutheran Joint Commission, *Baptists and Lutherans*

of the bilateral dialogues is the *Joint Declaration on the Doctrine of Justification* ratified by the Lutheran World Federation and the Roman Catholic Pontifical Council for Promoting Christian Unity in 1999.[18] In 2006, the World Methodist Council also became an official party to this consensus on a doctrine that divided the Western church in the Reformation.[19]

There have also been multilateral dialogues, conversations between representatives of three or more Christian communions, which have borne the fruit of convergence on divisive issues, even if not full visible unity. In 1982, the Faith and Order Commission of the World Council of Churches issued a convergence statement on *Baptism, Eucharist and Ministry* drafted by representatives of multiple Protestant denominations, the Eastern Orthodox churches, and the Roman Catholic Church.[20] Its commendation of

in Conversation: A Message to Our Churches (Gingins, Switzerland: Imprimerie La Colombiere SA, 1990); Mennonite World Conference and Baptist World Alliance, *Baptist-Mennonite Theological Conversations, 1989–1992: Final Report* (Nashville: Baptist World Alliance and Carol Stream, IL: Mennonite World Conference, 1992). Online: http://www.bwanet.org/media/documents/S&R-Baptist_Menonite_Theological_Conversations.pdf; Anglican Consultative Council and Baptist World Alliance, *Conversations Around the World, 2000–2005: The Report of the International Conversations between the Anglican Communion and the Baptist World Alliance* (London: Anglican Communion Office, 2005). Online: http://www.anglicancommunion.org/ministry/ecumenical/dialogues/baptist/docs/pdf/conversations_around_the_world.pdf.

18. Lutheran World Federation and Roman Catholic Church, *Joint Declaration on the Doctrine of Justification* (Grand Rapids: Eerdmans, 2000).

19. Geoffrey Wainwright, "World Methodist Council and the Joint Declaration on the Doctrine of Justification," *Pro Ecclesia* 16 (2007) 7–13.

20. World Council of Churches, *Baptism, Eucharist and Ministry*.

two legitimate patterns for uniting baptism, personal faith, and Christian education in the churches' work of making disciples has been the basis of much progress toward unity between churches that baptize only believers who have embraced the faith of their own volition and churches that also baptize infants whom the church nurtures in faith. Multilateral dialogues of a different sort, church union conversations, have resulted in the merger of some denominations with diverse patterns of church life in a number of national contexts around the world. Appendix 1, "Resources for Ecumenical Engagement," provides information on print and Internet sources for texts related to these bilateral and multilateral dialogues.

THE CURRENT ECUMENICAL IMPASSE

A century ago it would have been difficult to imagine the progress made in the quest for Christian unity in the past few decades. The first chapter of this book noted some of the reasons for these worries: a de-emphasis on the exploration of doctrine and church order in the World Council of Churches and the National Council of Churches of Christ in the USA, the passing of a gifted generation of ecumenical leadership, the internal divisions experienced by most denominations today, backlash against recent statements by the Vatican on the nature of the church, and the slowness with which the progress made in bilateral and multilateral dialogues has been received at the local level.

To this litany of lament over the current ecumenical situation should be added two additional factors. First, many within the segments of global Christianity that are thriving

Faith and Order Paper No. 111 (Geneva: WCC, 1982).

today, namely Evangelicalism and Pentecostalism, remain deeply suspicious of the ecumenical movement, especially of expressions of ecumenism that have anything to do with the World Council of Churches or the National Council of the Churches of Christ in the USA. They fear, occasionally with good reason, but often because of misimpressions and misinformation, that ecumenism means a lowest-common-denominator approach that compromises core convictions in the interest of securing a superficial unity. Yet Cardinal Walter Kasper (1933), head of the Pontifical Council for Promoting Christian Unity, represented the worldwide ecumenical movement at its best in his address in January 2008 on the occasion of the one-hundredth anniversary of the Week of Prayer for Christian Unity. He said,

> Ecumenical dialogue absolutely does not mean abandoning one's own identity in favor of an ecumenical "hotchpotch." It is a profound misunderstanding to see it as a form of compromising doctrinal relativism. The aim is not to find the lowest common denominator. Ecumenical dialogue aims not at spiritual impoverishment but at mutual spiritual enrichment. In ecumenical dialogue we discover the truth of the other as our own truth. So through the ecumenical dialogue the Spirit leads us into the whole truth; he heals the wounds of our divisions and bestows on us full catholicity.[21]

---

21. Walter Cardinal Kasper, "The Week of Prayer for Christian Unity: Origin and Continuing Inspiration of the Ecumenical Movement," in *A Century of Prayer for Christian Unity*, ed. Catherine E. Clifford (Grand Rapids: Eerdmans, 2009) 38.

In other words, "we're one, but we're not the same." Honestly addressing and coming to appreciate what makes us "not the same" can help the church become whole.

When Cardinal Kasper spoke of "catholicity," he wasn't talking about something that belongs already to the Roman Catholic Church but not yet to the other churches. When the early Christians applied to the church the Greek word *katholikē*, from which our word "catholic" comes and which meant both "universal" and "whole," they referred simultaneously to the universality of the church and to the wholeness or fullness of its faith and practice.[22] When some evangelical Christians hear the word "catholic" today, they immediately think of the Roman Catholic Church, which they may have been taught to regard as a false church that teaches a false gospel and has as its head a pope who holds a false office. On the basis of a certain way of reading the New Testament book of Revelation, they may also identify it as the "whore of Babylon" that in the last days will usher in a false one-world church and the Anti-Christ himself. Some who think in this way also see the ecumenical movement itself as preparing the way for this false one-world church. The persistence of a deeply entrenched anti-Catholicism, then, is a second additional factor that makes the quest for Christian unity seem humanly impossible right now.

The current ecumenical impasse does require a measure of realism on the part of everyone who longs for the unity of the church. But as Cardinal Kasper also said in the speech quoted above, "If it is true that the Holy Spirit initiated the ecumenical movement, then he will bring it also to

22. The earliest usage is Ignatius of Antioch (d. before 118) in his letter to the *Smyrneans* 8.2 (Bart D. Ehrman, ed. and trans., *The Apostolic Fathers* [Loeb Classical Library, no. 24; Cambridge: Harvard University Press, 2003] vol. 1, 305).

its goal."[23] That is the hope of ecumenism, and we should be confident in this hope, which chapter 5 will address more fully. In the meantime, "May the God of steadfastness and encouragement grant you to live in harmony with one another, in accordance with Christ Jesus, so that together you may with one voice glorify the God and father of our Lord Jesus Christ" (Rom 15:5–6).

23. Kasper, "Week of Prayer for Christian Unity," in *Century of Prayer*, ed. Clifford, 30.

3

One Life with Each Other

The Theology of Ecumenism

In light of all this, here's what I want you to do. While I'm locked up here, a prisoner for the Master, I want you to get out there and walk—better yet, run!—on the road God called you to travel. I don't want any of you sitting around on your hands. I don't want anyone strolling off, down some path that goes nowhere. And mark that you do this with humility and discipline—not in fits and starts, but steadily, pouring yourselves out for each other in acts of love, alert at noticing differences and quick at mending fences. You were all called to travel on the same road and in the same direction, so stay together, both outwardly and inwardly. You have one Master, one faith, one baptism, one God and Father of all, who rules over all, works through all, and is present in all. Everything you are and think and do is permeated with Oneness.

—Ephesians 4:1–6, *The Message*

THE MOST ENDURING DIVISION of American civil life and church life came into uncomfortably sharp focus during the 2008 Democratic presidential primary campaign.

Controversy over a widely circulated video clip of a sermon delivered shortly after September 11, 2001, by Rev. Jeremiah Wright, the retired pastor of Trinity United Church of Christ in Chicago, threatened to derail the campaign of Barak Obama. Regardless of one's political leanings, it was hard not to be moved by this key passage from the speech on race in America that then-Senator Obama delivered in response at the Constitution Center in Philadelphia on March 18, 2008. Obama said about his relationship with Rev. Wright:

> As imperfect as he may be, he has been like family to me. He strengthened my faith, officiated my wedding, and baptized my children. . . . I can no more disown him than I can disown the black community. I can no more disown him than I can my white grandmother—a woman who helped raise me, a woman who sacrificed again and again for me, a woman who loves me as much as she loves anything in this world, but a woman who once confessed her fear of black men who passed by her on the street, and who on more than one occasion has uttered racial or ethnic stereotypes that made me cringe. These people are a part of me.[1]

President Obama likely did not intend to make an authoritative theological pronouncement in that speech, yet he spoke truth about the nature of Christian unity—a truth that still stands, even though his eventual withdrawal of his membership from Trinity United Church of Christ when the connection became a seemingly insurmountable liability did not ideally embody the truth of his words. No matter how much we may disagree with or profoundly dislike some who profess to be followers of Christ, we cannot disown

1. Online: www.cnn.com/2008/POLITICS/03/18/obama.transcript.

them. They are family. They are part of us. As U2 sings in "One," we have "one life with each other, sisters, brothers." The bedrock theological principle of ecumenism is that the church is already one in Christ, for we are one body, the body of Christ. We're organically linked as members of one body and therefore members of one another. Our present divisions cannot undo that reality, but they can contradict that reality and obscure that reality from the watching world.

ONE GOD, ONE LORD, ONE CHURCH

The overarching theme of the New Testament letter to the Ephesians is the unity of the church as the body of Christ. It is part of God's plan to unify all things—"a plan for the fullness of time, to gather up all things in [Christ], things in heaven and things on earth" (1:10). As the body of Christ, the church is "the fullness of him who fills all in all" (1:22–23). The church is "one new humanity" that transcends Jew and Gentile—the ethnic divisions of humanity that mattered to the readers of this letter—in which both groups are reconciled "to God in one body through the cross" (2:15–16). Christian unity is no easy unity, for the church is a community in which we must "speak the truth to our neighbors, for we are members of one another" and in which we may need to "be angry" at one another while avoiding letting that anger turn into sin (4:25–26). Being members of the one body of Christ means to "be subject to one another out of reverence for Christ" (5:21–33).

At the center of this letter about the church's unity in Christ is chapter 4, verses 1–6. Much of what needs to be said about the theology of ecumenism can be said on the basis of these six verses. They make it clear that seeking the unity of the church is an unavoidable obligation of the Christian life. They specify how to live out that obligation in our relations with one another. And they identify the unifying realities of the faith that are the source of our unity and the resource for maintaining it.

A LIFE THAT LEADS TO UNITY

Theology at its best is not about abstract ideas. It does offer an intellectual account of the living story of Christian faith, but it also deals with the practices that embody this faith and the character of the people shaped by these practices. The first three chapters of Ephesians have told the story of God's saving work, which has the whole world in mind and which has as its focal point the cross of Christ, by which God reconciles divided humanity into one body. Now the remainder of the letter turns to the practices that live out this story. The whole of the Pauline Epistles' teaching on ethics—how Christians ought to practice their faith—can be summarized with this command: "Become what you are!"[2] That command presupposes a basic early Christian understanding of the "already" and "not yet" dimensions of the Christian faith. In Christ, we're already redeemed—but our earthly lives aren't fully there yet.

As the body of Christ, we do already share one life with each other. The unity of the church is already ours. But our divisions are evidence that this unity isn't yet fully realized, and so Ephesians turns to the practices and personal character that embody the church's oneness. "I . . . beg you to lead

2. This interpretation was advanced by Rudolf Bultmann, *Theology of the New Testament*, trans. Kendrick Grobel (New York: Scribner's, 1951) vol. 1, 332–33, but it has been echoed by numerous other interpreters of the Pauline literature in the New Testament.

a life worthy of the calling to which you have been called" (v. 1). The church can live out our one life with each other if we embody what the church already is in our relations with one another.

What sort of character, what sort of conduct toward each other embodies the church's calling as the unified body of Christ? According to verses 2 and 3, our one life with each other should be marked by two character traits and two practices.

Humility and Unity

We embody one life with each other through the character trait of humility. The two words translated "humility" and "gentleness" in the New Revised Standard Version were really synonyms in the Greek language. In English we'd call that a redundancy, but in Greek rhetoric the piling up of synonyms gave emphasis to an idea—what linguists call "semantic pleonasm," for those who care about such things. If "humility" and "gentleness" mean the same thing in the Greek employed here, the language is emphatically making the single point, "be utterly humble." Humility in the service of the unity of the church means being willing to contemplate the possibility that other Christians from whom we're divided may have preserved some conviction or practice belonging to the wholeness of the church's faith that our own church currently lacks, even while humbly offering the distinctive gifts of our own church to the rest of the body of Christ. Ecumenical humility means being open to the possibility that our own tradition could prove to be on the wrong side of this or that church-dividing issue, even while remaining committed to seeking the good of our own communion.

Patience and Unity

We embody one life with each other also through the character trait of patience. Patience is an indispensable ecumenical virtue, if for no other reason than that progress toward visible unity happens over centuries, even millennia. Unity is ultimately the gift of God, and when visible unity comes to pass it will be through the surprising work of the Holy Spirit. Humanly speaking, it's unlikely that full communion will happen in the lifetime of anyone engaged in the quest for Christian unity today. In a forum on dialogue between Catholics, Methodists, and Baptists sponsored by a student group at Duke Divinity School in Durham, North Carolina in March 2008, veteran Methodist ecumenist Geoffrey Wainwright said this:

> I used to say that I expected to end my ministry in communion with the Bishop of Rome without having become a Roman Catholic. I'm not planning now to live that long. Things have moved more slowly than in our initial enthusiasm and hope we thought, but they have moved. And it may well be that in fifty or a hundred or two hundred years or three hundred years, maybe, they will say, "Ah we wouldn't have achieved this unity without those people in the late twentieth and early twenty-first century." And more than that, I can't say. . . . But I do believe that we have the charge laid upon us by our Lord himself to live as one in him so that the world may know that he was sent by the Father as the Savior.[3]

3. "What do Methodists, Baptists, and Catholics Have in Common?" (Panel Discussion, Baptist House of Studies, Duke Divinity School, Durham, North Carolina, March 18, 2008; audio online: www.divinity.duke.edu/programs/baptisthouse/studentlife/document_view).

That kind of patience is tough for those of us who like to see tangible results, but our role model for patience is the God who is patient toward us, "merciful and gracious, slow to anger and abounding in steadfast love" (Ps 103:8). God has been at the business of seeking unity in God's divided church a little longer than we have, and God hasn't given up on it.

Putting Up with One Another

We embody one life with each other through the practice of "bearing with one another." "Bearing with one another" suggests something like "putting up with one another," the way we put up with family members whom we love but who thoroughly annoy us or with whom we have hotly-argued disagreements. It is the qualifier "in love" that makes putting up with one another possible, whether in family life or church life or in any of our relationships. Love in the biblical sense of the word makes putting up with each other possible because it is not a fleeting feeling that depends on whether we like the other or whether the other seems to love us. Love can be commanded in Scripture because love is an act of the will and not merely an emotion. When Jesus commands us, "love your enemies" (Matt 5:44), he's not saying "have warm feelings of affection for your enemies," but rather "love your enemies in the same way I love the people who crucified me and for whose sins I have died." If that's true for our relations with our enemies and with those currently outside the church, how much more should it be true of our relations with all those who belong to the body of Christ—even those we believe have dangerously distorted understandings of what it means to be Christian? We're urged to speak the

truth to one another later in chapter 4, and sometimes that
may tragically mean maintaining some of the current divisions of the church until we make more progress together
in our effort to "try to find out what is pleasing to the Lord"
(Eph 5:10).

I belong to the Region At-Large of the National
Association of Baptist Professors of Religion, a group of
Baptist professors of theology and religious studies that
meets annually in conjunction with the College Theology
Society, a gathering of Roman Catholic professors. Near the
end of each year's meeting we share in a common worship
service, a celebration of the Mass. Because as Baptists we are
not in communion with the bishop of Rome and because we
have what Catholicism regards as a defective understanding of what happens in the Eucharist, the Baptist professors
aren't permitted to receive the Eucharist during Mass. Instead
we receive a blessing from the priest at the altar in place of
bread and wine. Conversely, if our Catholic colleagues were
to attend a Baptist worship service that celebrated the Lord's
Supper, Catholic canon law would not permit them to receive communion with us, for in Catholic understanding
our celebrations of the Supper are not truly the Eucharist.
All of us gathered for worship at these meetings, Catholics
as well as Baptists, grieve the divisions manifested publicly
in our separation at the Lord's table, even while we rejoice
that we're able to participate together in other acts of worship during the Mass. We must bear with one another in
love, put up with one another in love, despite being hurt by
the other's exclusion of us. Such experiences of the woundedness of the body of Christ should spur us on in our efforts
to seek unity. If we do not bear with one another in love, our
woundedness will only reinforce our divisions.

Actively Maintaining Unity

We also embody one life with each other through the practice of maintaining unity—"maintaining the unity of the Spirit in the bond of peace." The choice of words is important here. The text doesn't say, "make unity happen" or "create some unity"; it says, "maintain unity." This could also be translated "safeguarding" or "preserving" or "holding on to" unity. Unity is God's gift entrusted to us—it is "the unity of the Spirit," which is simultaneously a unity that comes from the Spirit and a unity that characterizes the very life of the Spirit. According to the early Christian minister and theologian Augustine of Hippo (354–430), the Spirit is the bond of mutual love that unites Father, Son, and Spirit in the one life of the Triune God.[4] When the Spirit is at work in the church, the Spirit is fostering among us the very unity that belongs to God the Holy Trinity. It's our task to guard that unity, to preserve it, to keep it safe from harm.

It's hard to watch a half-hour of television without seeing at least two commercials for home security services. The security services industry in the United States recently reported annual revenues of $13.5 billion.[5] If we're willing to shell out that much money to protect our earthly possessions, how much more should we invest ourselves in guarding an infinitely more precious spiritual possession? God has given us unity as the body of Christ. The sacred

4. Augustine of Hippo *On the Trinity* 17.27—18.32 (*Nicene and Post-Nicene Fathers*, First Series, ed. Philip Schaff [New York: Christian Literature, 1887] 3:215–17).

5. "Security Systems Services," in *Encyclopedia of American Industries* (Farmington Hills, MI: Gale, 2008); reproduced in Business and Company Resource Center (Farmington Hills, MI: Gale, 2008) document no. I2501400875.

duty of every follower of Christ is to engage in the practice of maintaining that unity. The next chapter of this book will suggest ten specific things you can do to take up the practice of maintaining the unity of the church.

THE SOURCES OF TRUE UNITY

These traits and practices of unity have their source and motivation in the unifying realities of the faith identified in verses 4–6. We are "one body." There is only one Christ, and there is only one body of Christ. "Has Christ been divided?" Paul asks in 1 Cor 1:13, addressing divisions in the church at Corinth. To devote our energies to perpetuating our divisions is to betray our identity as the one body of Christ.

One Triune God

We share "one Spirit"—and also "one Lord" and "one God and Father of all." In other words, we share in common our devotion to the Triune God, which is the understanding of who God is that distinguishes Christianity from all other religious concepts of the divine. Even the World Council of Churches—a doctrinally diverse Christian organization if ever there was one—specifies the Trinitarian faith as the minimal doctrinal basis of Christian unity.[6] It is a doctrine we share across our divided traditions, and we do well to pay more attention to it. But the Triune God is not just a theological idea. The Trinity is nothing less than the divine life in which we participate and which participates in us, as we learned from Jesus's prayer in John 17 in the first chapter

6. "The Constitution and Rules of the World Council of Churches," appendix 11 in *The New Delhi Report: The Third Assembly of the World Council of Churches, 1961* (New York: Association, 1962) 426.

of this book. As we draw closer to the life of the Triune God, we also draw closer to one another.

The human dimension of our journey toward one another begins with our recognition in the other of our one Spirit, our one Lord, our one God and Father. Many Pentecostal Christians are instinctively ecumenical in the way they relate to other Christians because they find it inconceivable to stand distant from someone in whom they recognize the fruit of the indwelling Spirit. The rest of the church should follow their lead. If we're divided from a community of Christians who know the Father of Jesus Christ as God, who follow Jesus as Lord, and who experience the work of the Holy Spirit, then we have an obligation to be in dialogue with and cooperate with that other community.

One Hope

We have "one hope." A core Christian conviction is the hope that despite the violence and suffering and injustice that makes it look as if evil is getting the upper hand in the present order of things, there will come a day when "the kingdom of this world is become the kingdom of our Lord and of his Christ, and he shall reign for ever and ever" (Rev 11:15, as made familiar by the "Hallelujah Chorus" from Handel's *Messiah*). Even if divided Christians have serious disagreements about what it might mean for the present order of things to be transformed in the direction of the reign of God, we share a common hope that the reign of God will transform this world. The quest for Christian unity involves seeking solidarity with one another in speaking out against and working against injustice in all its forms. Our one hope also involves the biblical image of the messianic banquet at which the divided people of God are finally fully united (Isa 25:6–8, Matt 22:1–14, Luke 13:29 and 14:7–24, Rev 19:9). Participating in the quest for Christian unity is itself a way of seeking that for which we hope.

One Faith

We also have "one faith." Faith is not simply intellectual assent, believing a set of ideas to be true. The biblical word "faith" has in mind something much more active. Faith is an active trust in God that involves faithfulness, and as we're reminded in chapter 2 of Ephesians, this faith is God's gift that brings about our salvation. We have in common this saving faith, and we must seek unity with all who share it. Faith also does have an intellectual dimension, and it is here that our divisions reveal the crippled nature of the church. As we do the work of forming Christians in the faith, we aren't yet able to teach one faith, and so the teaching ministry of the divided church perpetuates the church's divisions. But the answer isn't to dispense with doctrine as being inherently divisive. There is one shared faith taught by the church, and it is found in the story of the Triune God that is told at length and with great specificity in the Bible and that is summarized in the ancient creeds like the Apostles' Creed and the Nicene Creed, which teach in brief what the Bible teaches at length. If we can reclaim the centrality of these doctrines of the faith that we ought to share as one faith, we may be in a better position for making progress together on those doctrines that continue to divide us.

One Baptism

We share "one baptism." There is only one baptism because when we are baptized, we are baptized into the body of Christ and not into a denomination or into a local church. Yet our baptisms are performed by local churches that identify with particular denominational traditions, so our baptisms are paradoxical: we are simultaneously baptized into the one body of Christ and into the current divisions of the church. One of the most pressing ecumenical issues today is the mutual recognition of one another's baptisms. If there is only one baptism into the one body of Christ, then there's a sense in which not to recognize the baptism of another church as a legitimate baptism is to say, "your church is not really a church," and if the other church is not really a church, then that is also to say, "and you're not really a Christian."[7] Much progress has been made in this area. Chapter 2 of this book mentioned the 1982 *Baptism, Eucharist and Ministry* document issued by the World Council of Churches. This text has been widely influential as a model for ecumenical convergence on the recognition of one baptism, but much work remains to be done before we can live out in practice the unifying reality of the one baptism we share.

Baptism does change the nature of reality. Baptism makes sisters and brothers out of strangers. Baptism creates a new family that takes precedence over the relationships we have with the families that include parents, siblings, spouses, and children. When President Obama said that his former pastor was "like family" to him, that he couldn't disown him

7. Thanks to Curtis W. Freeman for many conversations in which he has helped me and many others appreciate the logical implications of this insistence of some churches on re-baptizing candidates for membership who have already been baptized in other communions.

because he was part of him, he was precisely right. Yet many of us have gotten too comfortable with avoiding being identified with other Christians with whom we strongly disagree. My own Baptist denomination has been through some very bitter and very public controversies during that past couple of decades, and as a result many of us find ourselves explaining to other people, "I'm a Baptist, but not *that* kind of a Baptist." In a book on Baptist identity, British Baptist theologian Paul Fiddes mentions some examples of this "I'm like these Baptists/I'm not like those Baptists" approach to Baptist identity, and then asks: "But does making a personal list of those who are to be approved as fellow Baptists make a community?"[8] The answer is of course no. Whether we like it or not, all who are the children of the heavenly Father through Christ and in the Spirit belong to us, and we belong to them. They are family; we cannot disown them. The theology of ecumenism set forth in Ephesians 4 teaches us that. So does the same theology set to music in "The Church's One Foundation" by the nineteenth-century Anglican priest and hymn writer Samuel John Stone (1839–1900). That classic hymn tune sounded amazingly contemporary when an auditorium full of college students, led by two vocalists and accompanied by two acoustic guitars, sang it at the conclusion of the lecture on which this chapter is based. Its text is startlingly relevant to the ecumenical situation today, too:

> The Church's one foundation
> is Jesus Christ her Lord;
> she is his new creation,
> by water and the word:
> from heaven he came and sought her
> to be his holy bride;

8. Paul S. Fiddes, *Tracks and Traces: Baptist Identity in Church and Theology*, Studies in Baptist History and Thought, vol. 13) Milton Keynes, UK: Paternoster, 2003) 13.

with his own blood he bought her,
and for her life he died.

Elect from every nation,
yet one o'er all the earth,
her charter of salvation,
one Lord, one faith, one birth;
one holy Name she blesses,
partakes one holy food,
and to one hope she presses,
with every grace endued.

Though with a scornful wonder
men see her sore oppressed,
by schisms rent asunder,
by heresies distressed;
yet saints their watch are keeping,
their cry goes up, "How long?"
and soon the night of weeping
shall be the morn of song.

Mid toil and tribulation,
and tumult of her war
she waits the consummation
of peace for evermore;
till with the vision glorious
her longing eyes are blessed,
and the great Church victorious
shall be the Church at rest.

Yet she on earth hath union
with God, the Three in one,
and mystic sweet communion
with those whose rest is won.
O happy ones and holy!
Lord, give us grace that we
like them, the meek and lowly,
on high may dwell with thee.[9]

9. Samuel John Stone, "The Church's One Foundation" (1868). Online:
www.oremus.org/hymnal/t/t093.html.

As the hymn text suggests, the saints gone before are not only watching our continuation of their struggle for the unity of the church. These "happy ones and holy," among whom are the shapers of the quest for Christian unity named in chapter 2, provide us with examples of how to embody the "meek and lowly" ecumenical virtues of humility and patience, as well as how to engage in the ecumenical practices of bearing with one another and maintaining the unity of the church. They did so in the midst of all sorts of conflict. They pursued Christian unity in the midst of persecutions from without the church and the challenges of heresies and schisms from within, which did not deter them from pressing toward one hope. They sought the unity of the church in the face of discouraging evidence of its disunity because they were convinced that in Christ we already have one life with each other, rooted in the unifying realities set forth in Scripture and echoed in this hymn: one Christological foundation of the church, one baptism, one sacred Word, one saving sacrifice, one Lord, one faith, one birth, one name, one holy food, one hope, one holy Trinity, one communion of saints. They labored that the church might fully embody what the church already has in Christ: "one life with each other, sisters, brothers." The next chapter suggests some concrete ways in which we might follow their example today.

4

Leaves You If You Don't Care for It

10 Things You Can Do for the Unity of the Church

> The way God designed our bodies is a model for understanding our lives together as a church: every part dependent on every other part, the parts we mention and the parts we don't, the parts we see and the parts we don't. If one part hurts, every other part is involved in the hurt, and in the healing. If one part flourishes, every other part enters into the exuberance. You are Christ's body—that's who you are! You must never forget this. Only as you accept your part of that body does your "part" mean anything.
>
> —1 Corinthians 12:25–27, *The Message*

ACCORDING TO EPHESIANS 4:3, one of the practices that worthily embodies the vocation (calling) of all Christians is the practice of maintaining the unity of the church—safeguarding, preserving, holding on to the unity already entrusted to us by God. There's a line in U2's song "One" that speaks to this practice: "One love—we get to share it/it leaves you baby if you don't care for it." The love that belongs to a marriage or a friendship doesn't endure all by itself. It requires maintenance. Both parties in a relationship have to contribute something to the deepening of the relationship as an intentional, ongoing practice; otherwise the relationship's already on its way to dissolution. It leaves you if you don't care for it.

EVERY CHRISTIAN AN ECUMENIST

This chapter turns to the practical matters of grassroots ecumenical involvement. For too long, ecumenism has been perceived as something that concerned only theologians and those at the highest levels of church and denominational leadership. Unfortunately those who have this professional role in the quest for Christian unity haven't always done a good job of helping the lay membership of the churches understand that they, too, have a stake in the ecumenical movement and are in fact its most important participants.

It's important that all members of the church learn about the ecumenical movement and what it has to do with them, but for the sake of the future of the church and its unity it is especially crucial that the generation of younger Christians now in college, entering the workplace, and beginning their adult participation in the life of their churches catch this vision and put it into practice. Here are ten specific things younger Christians can do to take up the practice of maintaining the unity of the church. These actions aren't restricted to the chronologically young, however, for the future of the ecumenical movement will also be shaped by those who are young in spirit. Ephesians 4:3 applies to all members of the church, and any member of the church can do these ten things.

PRAYING FOR UNITY

First, pray for the unity of the church. We learn to pray
from Jesus, and in John 17 Jesus models for us the practice
of praying for Christian unity. If unity is the gift of God,
if full visible unity will come about in Christ's own time
and in Christ's own way, if progress toward visible unity
depends on the surprising work of the Holy Spirit among
us, then praying that God might make us one is the most
significant thing any Christian can do to further the cause
of Christian unity. Each January 18–25 there is a Week
of Prayer for Christian Unity, which celebrated the one-
hundredth anniversary of its founding in 2008. Founded by
an American Episcopal priest named Paul Watson in 1908,
today churches from all denominations worldwide join in
this observance. If your congregation hasn't yet observed the
Week of Prayer for Christian Unity, the Franciscan Friars of
the Atonement make planning resources freely available on
the Internet.[1] But praying for unity ought not be limited to
one week a year. There are daily cycles of World Prayer for
churches of all denominations in all nations also available
on the Internet, and these can be followed in private prayer
and public worship as a means of seeking the good of other
Christians in other denominations and reminding ourselves
of our connections to them.[2]

---

1. Online: www.atonementfriars.org/week_of_prayer.htm.

2. For example, the Ecumenical Prayer Cycle provided by the World
Council of Churches (Online: www.oikoumene.org/?id=3038). A
daily World Cycle of Prayer for the churches of the world's nations and
Denominational Cycle of Prayer for specific Christian communions are
incorporated into the Online Daily Office maintained by the Mission of
St. Clare (Online: www.missionstclare.com/english).

Second, pray for the unity of the church in the company of other Christians with whom you have serious disagreements. In 2006, I participated in two different sorts of conferences related to the quest for Christian unity. In January 2006, I was a member of a consultation convened by the Foundation for a Conference on Faith and Order in North America that met for three days at the Graymoor Ecumenical and Interreligious Institute in Garrison, New York. The purpose of the consultation was primarily to examine the factors behind the failure of plans for an envisioned Second Conference on Faith and Order in North America that would revisit the 1957 Oberlin conference on "The Nature of the Unity We Seek" in connection with the fiftieth anniversary of that gathering. This time, it was hoped, there would be broader participation by Roman Catholic and evangelical churches beyond the mainline Protestant establishment than was the case at that significant milestone in the development of North American ecumenism, yet it was not to be—at least not in 2007. The secondary purpose of the consultation was to contemplate the possibilities for such a conference in the future. While some of the presentations and discussions evidenced a remarkable degree of ecumenical energy among the constituencies represented at the consultation, the gathering seemed like a funeral for the death of an ecumenical dream. And yet when we joined in common worship each morning and evening, singing Taizé chants and praying together for the unity of the church, we experienced the rekindling of a hope that didn't seem warranted by the circumstances.

In December 2006, I served as a member of the Baptist World Alliance delegation to the first round of a new five-year series of conversations with the Pontifical Council for

Promoting Christian Unity that met at Samford University's Beeson Divinity School in Birmingham, Alabama. In contrast to the Graymoor consultation, the mood of these conversations was far from somber, yet all participants were acutely aware of the inevitable ecclesiological impasses that lay ahead. Even so, when the delegates gathered for morning and evening prayer each day in Beeson Divinity School's Hodges Chapel, where Thomas Aquinas and Martin Luther significantly stand side-by-side facing worshipers among the sixteen representatives of the communion of saints whose frescoes encircle the chapel's dome, those who were not yet able to be united at the Lord's table were nevertheless able to be united in praying together along with their Lord that they might one day be made one. That experience embodied a principle of praying for unity set forth by Dom Olivier Rousseau of the Eastern Rite Catholic monastery in Chevetogne and summarized here by the co-authors of a helpful introduction to ecumenism:

> [C]rossconfessional communal prayer for unity is grounded in the promise that the prayer of two or three gathered in Jesus' name will be answered (Matthew 18:19–20). During their prayer those gathered are not divided. These moments of unity become, as it were, an apprenticeship in the more pervasive unity for which those gathered are praying. These moments of prayer move Christians from being persons whose backs are turned towards each other, each confession facing away from the others, to Christians turned toward God and one another, beginning to recognize themselves as disciples of the same Lord. The act of gathering in Jesus' name to pray for unity is a moment of such unity.[3]

3. Gros, McManus, and Riggs, *Introduction to Ecumenism*, 104.

Do you have personal friends who attend churches of different denominations? Invite them to pray with you sometime for the unity of your churches. Suggest to members of your own congregation that they invite members of a neighboring congregation of another denomination to meet regularly to pray together for Christian unity. Such experiences of praying for unity at the boundaries of the church's divisions provide a way to embody now the unity we already have in Christ, even while confessing the sinfulness of our divisions and asking God to guide us in doing what we need to do to heal them.

EMBRACING THE CHURCH—AND ITS DIVISIONS

Third, commit yourself to the life of a particular church, warts and all. The first chapter noted that many Christian young adults today frequently worship with multiple congregations, often of differing denominations. That trend serves as evidence that young adults already have some ecumenical instincts that can lead them to become more intentionally involved in the quest for Christian unity. On the other hand, that trend also worries me a bit, because we grow in Christ by being accountable to a specific group of fellow believers with whom we worship and pray and share the Lord's table, who shape us by the example of their lives, who along with us are the presence of Christ in a particular community. Christian unity begins with the unity of the local church, and the unity of the local church is not well served when we follow our shifting preferences from church to church or when we quickly leave one church for another when someone offends us or we disagree with a minister or we don't like how worship is done there. We learn the cruciform practice of Christian unity, of "bearing with one another in love" (Eph 4:3), by remaining in fellowship with a specific body of Christians in spite of its faults, and even in spite of the sins of some of its members against us.

Fourth, embrace a particular denominational tradition. This one is a little counterintuitive. It might seem that the best way to seek the unity of the church is to become a "non-denominational" Christian. While there are churches that call themselves non-denominational churches, there's really no such thing. As soon as a supposedly non-denominational church has made decisions about what happens in worship, whom and how they will baptize, how and with what understanding they will celebrate holy communion, what they will teach, who their ministers will be and how they will be ordained, or how they will relate to other churches, these decisions have placed the church within the stream of a specific type of denominational tradition. The way to unity is not to leave particular denominational traditions behind, but rather to embrace them. The denominations are divided, but each also has historic connections to the church's catholicity, which chapter 2 defined as the wholeness or fullness of faith and practice that belongs to the whole church. We can make progress toward unity when we recover catholicity within the denominations, and we make progress toward unity when the denominations share their distinctive patterns of catholicity with one another. As individual Christians, we must be shaped by a particular denominational tradition in order to help our own church toward unity and in order to help the rest of the church learn from our own church.

Fifth, learn all you can about the "Great Tradition" to which all denominational traditions are heirs. Long before there was a Protestant Reformation and prior to the schism between Roman Catholicism and Eastern Orthodoxy, there was a millennium of Christianity from the end of the New Testament era to the early Middle Ages that preceded the current divisions of the church. The faith and practice of this ancient, more united church is what many have taken to calling the "Great Tradition." Catholic, Orthodox, and Protestant Christians of all stripes have this Great Tradition as their common heritage. It is a heritage that includes the canon of Scripture, the early ecumenical creeds, the writings of the early church fathers and mothers, and the patterns and practices of ancient Christian worship. The Great Tradition is not alien to our denominational traditions, for in various ways they depend on it and continue it. But our journeys of development as separate denominations have sometimes loosened our roots in the Great Tradition. Recovering the Great Tradition we share in common can facilitate our movement toward full visible unity with one another. In recent years several evangelical historians and theologians have published a number of accessible books aimed at popular readerships that can introduce you to the Great Tradition and its relevance to the church of today.[4] If

4. E.g., James S. Cutsinger, ed., *Reclaiming the Great Tradition: Evangelicals, Catholics and Orthodox in Dialogue* (Downers Grove: InterVarsity, 1997); Christopher A. Hall, *Reading Scripture with the Church Fathers* (Downers Grove: InterVarsity, 1998); Robert Webber, *Ancient-Future Faith: Rethinking Evanglicalism for a Postmodern World* (Grand Rapids: Baker, 1999); D. H. Williams, *Retrieving the Tradition and Renewing Evangelicalism: A Primer for Suspicious Protestants* (Grand Rapids: Eerdmans, 1999); Stephen Holmes, *Listening to the Past: The Place of Tradition in Theology* (Grand Rapids: Baker, 2002); D. H. Williams, ed., *The Free Church and the Early Church: Bridging the Historical and Theological Divide* (Grand Rapids: Eerdmans, 2002); Steven R. Harmon, *Towards Baptist Catholicity: Essays on Tradition and the Baptist Vision* (Milton Keynes, UK: Paternoster, 2006); Bryan M. Litfin, *Getting to*

you are currently a university student, you may be able to take courses that can help you learn about the history of the church that preceded your own.

Sixth, learn all you can about other denominational traditions. The study of church history isn't just for those preparing for ordained ministry at seminaries and divinity schools. One church historian calls church history "the history of us all,"[5] and if that's true all Christians have a stake in learning about it. Books, college courses, and congregation-based studies on church history can introduce you not only to the Great Tradition but also to the other denominational traditions that developed out of it. Chapter 2 mentioned the ecumenical dialogues that have taken place between denominational traditions during the past forty years. Many of those dialogues have resulted in the publication of joint statements that recount the stories of the two denominations in relation to one another and identify major areas of agreement between them as well as the points of continued disagreement. Sometimes they propose practical steps that can be taken at the local level to enhance unity between the two denominations. If your own denomination has been in

---

Know the Church Fathers: An Evangelical Introduction (Grand Rapids: Brazos, 2007); and the volumes issued thus far in the series Evangelical *Ressourcement*: Ancient Sources for the Church's Future, edited by D. H. Williams and published by Baker Academic: D. H. Williams, *Evangelicals and Tradition: The Formative Influence of the Early Church* (2005); idem, ed., *Tradition, Scripture, and Interpretation: A Sourcebook of the Ancient Church* (2006); Craig D. Allert, *A High View of Scripture: The Authority of the Bible and the Formation of the New Testament Canon* (2007); Ronald E. Heine, *Reading the Old Testament with the Ancient Church: Exploring the Formation of Early Christian Thought* (2007).

5. E. Glenn Hinson, "Some Things I've Learned from the Study of Early Christian History," *Review and Expositor* 101 (2004) 739.

this kind of official dialogue with other churches, studying and discussing these reports would be an ideal way to learn about other denominations and their relationship to your own tradition.

Mary Reath, an Episcopal layperson, attended a study course that introduced the ecumenical initiatives between the churches of the Anglican Communion and the Roman Catholic Church. The course excited her about these developments in relationships between the Roman Catholic communion of her upbringing and the Episcopal church of her adult life, and she became eager to share this information with others. But she quickly discovered that little had been written about it with laypeople in mind, so she wrote a book herself to meet that need.[6] There is a desperate need for more ecumenical literature that, like Reath's book, introduces the laity of the churches to the dialogues and agreements that affect them and ought to involve them. In the meantime, laypersons can read the agreed statements issued by the dialogues and discuss them with their ministers and with one another. The first appendix to this book, "Resources for Ecumenical Engagement," provides information about print and Internet sources for these texts.

Seventh, while remaining committed to your own denominational tradition, adopt another denominational tradition as a second tradition, much as you would learn a second language. I make this suggestion with great caution. Don't even think about pursuing recommendation number seven without first investing your time and energy in working on recommendation number four—which was,

---

6. Mary Reath, *Rome & Cantuerbury: The Elusive Search for Unity* (Lanham, MD: Rowman & Littlefield, 2007).

"embrace a particular denominational tradition." Otherwise your Christian formation might be a little like what your ability to communicate might be if around age three you quit learning English but then learned only bits and pieces of a second language. But just as learning a second language after you have mastered your own can give you not only the ability to communicate with someone from another culture but also an appreciation for their culture and the capacity to share with that person what is distinctive about your own culture, so it is with what I cautiously suggest here. If you are well-grounded in a denominational tradition and continue to be actively involved in the worship, work, and witness of a specific local church belonging to that tradition, there's no substitute for learning about another denomination by intentionally and regularly participating in its worship and taking up its practices of personal devotion.

As a Baptist seminary student I began to do this with the Anglican tradition. I would attend services of morning and evening prayer or Sunday Eucharistic services whenever I had the opportunity, especially when traveling, and I followed the cycle of readings for morning and evening prayer from the *Book of Common Prayer* for my own devotions. That has given me an appreciation for another tradition that has enriched my own Baptist faith. I've incorporated into my Baptist pattern of faith and practice some of the gifts the Anglican tradition has to offer, but my experience of the other tradition has also made me more keenly aware of the gifts that belong distinctively to my Baptist tradition and has helped me treasure them. It also equipped me for serving as a member of the Baptist delegation to the North American phase of the international theological conversations between the Baptist World Alliance and the Anglican Consultative Council in 2003.[7]

Over time, becoming "bi-denominational"—participating in the life of another church communion even while remaining a committed member of your own denomination—can equip you for serving as something of a mediator between the traditions. This seems to be the sort of ecumenical practice that the drafters of the *Princeton Proposal for Christian Unity*, issued in 2003, had in mind in section 55 of that document:

> When full communion does not exist, churches should acknowledge and encourage special vocations for the sake of unity. God may call lay and ordained members of one church to sustained participation in the life and mission of separated churches, even if sacramental communion is not possible for a time. Such vocations do not deny real theological differences or disrespect canonical order but rather are a call to endure separation as a discipline which sharpens passion for unity. Such sacrifice is perhaps possible only for a few, and it will certainly take many forms, often partial and hidden. The churches should seek to identify and champion these vocations as a gift of the Holy Spirit to the divided churches.[8]

7. Anglican Consultative Council and Baptist World Alliance, *Conversations Around the World, 2000–2005: The Report of the International Conversations between the Anglican Communion and the Baptist World Alliance* (London: Anglican Communion Office, 2005). Online: http://www.anglicancommunion.org/ministry/ecumenical/dialogues/baptist/docs/pdf/conversations_around_the_world.pdf.

8. Carl E. Braaten and Robert W. Jenson, eds., *In One Body Through the Cross: The Princeton Proposal for Christian Unity. A Call to the Churches from an Ecumenical Study Group* (Grand Rapids: Eerdmans, 2003) 49–50.

This particular ecumenical practice may not be for everyone, but those who take it up may find themselves uniquely positioned for helping members of their own church to understand more fully the other denomination and for helping Christians they meet in the other denominational context come to understand their own "home" tradition. "Bi-denominational" Christians can be key facilitators of the exchange of ecclesial gifts among the divided churches.

COMING TOGETHER—SHARING, SERVING, STUDYING

Eighth, join other Christians in sharing the good news of Jesus Christ in word and deed. The modern ecumenical movement began among missionaries, and joining together with Christians from other denominations in living out the Great Commission continues to be a key contribution to the unity of the church. Some readers of this book may have already become involved in doing that through interdenominational campus organizations like InterVarsity Christian Fellowship or Campus Crusade for Christ. There are also possibilities for linking ecumenical cooperation in evangelism to your participation in the life of a local church. Are you involved in making plans for a church mission trip or a church-sponsored Habitat for Humanity project? Suggest to others in your church the possibility of inviting the ministers and membership of a nearby church from a different denomination to be part of the team for the trip or project. Will your church be involved in an intentional effort to share the good news with your community and to invite its residents to visit your church? Suggest to those planning for such an evangelistic effort that they invite churches of other denominations in the community to be part of that project. Coming together to offer to the world the one faith we share demonstrates to the world the unity we have in Christ, and the deep experiences of unity that can result will push us to go to work on the issues that continue to divide us at the Lord's table.

Ninth, join other Christians in serving as advocates for social justice and environmental responsibility. It may be that the first large-scale grassroots embodiment of the modern ecumenical movement in the United States was the civil rights movement. Christians who had never worshiped together and who in some cases couldn't have gathered around the Lord's table together had deep experiences of Christian unity when they worked together, Protestant and Catholic, black and white, in marches and demonstrations and voter registration drives. Some have called this an "ecumenism of the trenches." More recently this kind of experience has led to the formation of a group called Evangelicals and Catholics Together, which involves a number of Catholic and evangelical scholars and church leaders who are not officially representing their churches but who meet together regularly to discuss some of the pressing social issues of the day and to publish statements of their common convictions.[9]

9. Charles W. Colson and Richard John Neuhaus, eds., *Evangelicals and Catholics Together: Toward a Common Mission* (Dallas: Word, 1995); "The Gift of Salvation: A Statement of Evangelicals and Catholics Together," *First Things* (January 1998). Online: www.firstthings.com/article.php3?id_article=3453; "Your Word Is Truth: A Statement of Evangelicals and Catholics Together," *First Things* (August/September 2002). Online: www.firstthings.com/article.php3?id_article=2058; "The Communion of Saints: A Statement of Evangelicals and Catholics Together," *First Things* (March 2003). Online: www.firstthings.com/article.php3?id_article=459; "The Call to Holiness: A Statement of Evangelicals

The threats to human life and its dignity and the destruction of God's good creation that result from human sinfulness provide all of us with opportunities to join other Christians in doing something about it. Those efforts also make their own contributions to the quest for Christian unity.

Tenth, in connection with all the above: search the Scriptures—devotionally, in the context of corporate worship, and with study groups in your own congregation, but also with Christians from other traditions. The foundation of the Great Tradition is the Bible itself. The canon of Scripture, the books of the Old and New Testaments regarded by the church as authoritative in matters of faith and practice, developed out of the early controversies over key issues of Christian faith that led to important clarifications of the faith we share in common. Allowing for some variation in the books that make up the Old Testament, Protestants share the Bible in common with Roman Catholic and Eastern Orthodox Christians. We will be better prepared for making individual contributions to Christian unity if we first know well our common source of authority.

We also ought to seek opportunities for studying the Scriptures with Christians from other denominations—and we ought not to shy away from the conflicts that may arise when we do so. In a class discussion a few years ago, one of my former students reported participating in a parachurch program for interdenominational Bible study that requires that those who attend the Bible studies not mention anything about what their denomination teaches about the meaning

---

and Catholics Together," *First Things* (March 2005). Online: www.first-things.com/article.php3?id_article=171; "That They May Have Life: A Statement of Evangelicals and Catholics Together," *First Things* (October 2006). Online: www.firstthings.com/article.php3?id_article=5358.

of the Scriptures, supposedly in the interest of maintaining unity. I understand the motivation for that, but I disagree. The perspectives on the Bible we share with each other *are* shaped by our churches, and we need to own up to that so we can learn not only from one another but also from one another's churches. Moving toward unity requires that we not only come to an appreciation of each other's faith; it also requires that we contest our serious disagreements with one another in love. Moral philosopher Alasdair MacIntyre defines a "living tradition" as one in which there is an ongoing argument about the good that constitutes that tradition. Without that ongoing argument, the tradition is either dying or already dead.[10] If that's true of the living tradition that is the Christian tradition, then we're all engaged in an ongoing argument about the meaning of our agreed authority for faith and practice, the Bible. The health of the church as a living tradition depends on our reading the Scriptures together and earnestly contesting their meaning. That happens best when the divided traditions come together; it can't happen easily when we read the Bible apart from one another.

Unity is God's gift. It leaves us, or more accurately we leave it, if we don't care for it. I pray that each of you who read this book will offer your own distinctive gifts in the service of the unity of the church, through Jesus Christ our Lord.

---

10. Alasdair MacIntyre, *After Virtue: A Study in Moral Theory*, 2nd ed. (Notre Dame, IN: University of Notre Dame Press, 1984) 222.

5

Hear Us Call

The Eschatology of Ecumenism

God, how long will it take . . . ?

—Psalm 6:3, *The Message*

I'm not saying that I have this all together, that I
have it made. But I am well on my way, reaching
out for Christ, who has so wondrously reached out
for me. Friends, don't get me wrong: By no means
do I count myself an expert in all of this, but I've
got my eye on the goal, where God is beckoning us
onward—to Jesus. I'm off and running, and I'm not
turning back.

—Philippians 3:12–14, *The Message*

THE QUEST FOR CHRISTIAN unity makes sense only
in light of its relation to what systematic theologians
call *eschatology*. Eschatology is the technical term for the
division of theology that deals with "last things," from the
Greek *eschatos* meaning "last," and the Greek *logos* meaning
"ordered thought" about something. But eschatology isn't
only about what happens at the end or some chronology of

end-time events. The Baptist theologian James Wm. McClendon Jr. defined eschatology much more broadly: it's "about what lasts; it is also about what comes last, and about the history that leads from the one to the other."[1] In other words, eschatology has to do with God's goals for all creation, from creation to consummation and everything in between. It also has to do with our participation in what God is doing to realize God's goals for all creation.

LIVING IN THE TENSION

Eschatology has often suffered from two extreme and inadequate perspectives on God's work in the world. A wholly realized eschatology has no need of a future hope: it has the fullness of salvation, "the power of his resurrection," now. It is quite satisfied with life as it is, with little place for "the sharing of his sufferings" (Phil 3:10) as a paradigm for the Christian life. On the other hand, a wholly future eschatology gives up on the present world as the arena of God's reconciling work. It waits instead for a new heaven and a new earth that are radically discontinuous with the present order. But the eschatology of the Bible as interpreted by the mainstream Christian tradition maintains a tension between the "already" and the "not yet." The reign of God is at hand and people already have the opportunity to participate in it in the here-and-now, but it is manifestly not yet fully realized because humanity doesn't yet fully participate in the reign of God. This tension between the "already" and the

1. James Wm. McClendon Jr., *Systematic Theology*, vol. 2, *Doctrine* (Nashville: Abingdon, 1994) 96. This is an expansion of an earlier definition offered by Paul Althaus, *Die Letzen Dinge: Lehrbuch der Eschatologie* (Gütersloh: Gerd Mohr, 1948) 29, according to which eschatology is about "what lasts" and "what comes last."

"not yet" is at the core of the doctrinal framework in light of which Christians make sense of the world, God's work in the world, the mission of the church, and the nature of the Christian life this side of heaven. Most significantly for the subject of this book, this eschatological tension is what makes sense of the quest for Christian unity and our own individual contributions to it. It also happens to be the key theological concept for understanding the spiritual significance of the whole of the music of U2. While the band may not have imagined that the artistic products of their reading of the world through Christian lenses would be put to such a use, it's not too much of a stretch to connect the eschatology embedded in the U2 catalog to the eschatology of ecumenism.

In the formative years of the band, U2 found a way to express this tension between the already and the not-yet dimensions of the reign of God musically, through the distinctive instrumental sound they created and quite apart from the lyrics. As guitarist The Edge recalls their early musical experimentation, "We didn't like major chords because they sounded too happy"—in other words, major chords communicated an overly realized eschatology—"and minor chords sounded too down"—that is, minor chords were eschatologically pessimistic. So The Edge dropped the third out of his chords—"the third became our enemy," he says—leaving the root, the fifth, and the octave of the root, and creating a sound neither obviously major nor obviously minor.[2] It's the sound of the already/not-yet eschatology of the Bible translated into the idiom of European post-punk

2. Bono, The Edge, Adam Clayton, and Larry Mullen Jr., *U2 by U2* (London: HarperCollins, 2006) 72.

rock music by a band with a Christian eschatological perspective on the world.

The classic expression of U2's eschatological outlook is "I Still Haven't Found What I'm Looking For" from *The Joshua Tree* (1987). The "already" dimension of Christian faith is stated in no uncertain terms: "You broke the bonds and you loosed the chains/carried the cross and all my shame." But even that has not yet completely transformed all that is wrong with the world (or the singer): "But I still haven't found what I'm looking for." On *How to Dismantle an Atomic Bomb* (2004) the song "Yahweh" voices a similar already-but-not-yet hope: "Always pain before a child is born ... Still I'm waiting for the dawn."

More recently, U2 has expressed this eschatology with an image. The cover of their 2009 album *No Line on the Horizon* was selected from a series of seascapes by Japanese photographer Hiroshi Sugimoto. Before the cover artwork was released to the public, it was widely rumored that it would feature the Sugimoto photograph "Ligurian Sea, Saviore," a seascape in which sea and sky blend into one another with no discernable boundary—no line on the horizon, suggestive of the full presence of the infinite, the union of heaven and earth. But in the end, the band settled on another Sugimoto image: "Boden Sea, Uttwil," in which, despite the album title, there *is* still a clear line on the horizon. The cover suggests something like "your kingdom come, your will be done, on earth as it is in heaven." Earth is not yet heaven, yet we pray and work for the day when things will fully be on earth as they are in heaven—when heaven and earth will be indistinguishable, and there will at last be no line on the horizon. It's a visual rendering of this already/not-yet eschatology, with the emphasis on the fact that the world has not yet been transformed into what comes last, the full realization of the reign of God.

WHAT LASTS—ALL THAT YOU CAN'T LEAVE BEHIND

At the same time, we have the opportunity to participate in what lasts, to practice the things that make a real difference in helping the world become what it will be at the last, right now. The hope that the not-yet-transformed aspects of this world can yet be changed by our participation in what God is already doing in the world is the premise of the numerous U2 songs that since their 1983 *War* album have named the injustices of the present order of things and called for the justice of the reign of God to be done in various contexts.

One of those songs, "Walk On" from *All That You Can't Leave Behind* (2000), was inspired by Aung San Suu Kyi's leadership of the Burmese people's non-violent resistance to the Myanmar military junta. While Suu Kyi is a Theravada Buddhist, her voluntary identification with the oppression of her people—which meant leaving behind her career, security, freedom, and life with her children and dying husband—profoundly illustrates the cruciform nature of the Christian life and its relation to what lasts. As The Edge intones at the beginning of "Walk On," "Love is not the easy thing . . . The only baggage you can bring/Is all that you can't leave behind." The promotional video the band filmed for the song in Rio de Janeiro, Brazil, intensifies the song's connections with cruciform love as the thing that lasts and brings about what comes last. The video opens with a close-up shot of a crucifix hanging from Bono's neck as he arises in his room in the Copacabana Palace Hotel. The main section of the video juxtaposes scenes of the life of adulation and ease enjoyed by the band on their visit to the city with images of the daily lives of the poor in its slums. Then as Bono sings an inventory of the sorts of things that fall short of the self-sacrificing love displayed in the cross—"all this you can leave behind"—the video moves toward its conclusion with a breathtaking aerial shot of the band ascending Corcovado Mountain to reach the Christ the Redeemer statue, which overlooks the city with arms outstretched in cruciform posture. Finally the scene shifts from this image of Christ and its suggestion of his cross to footage of Suu Kyi under house arrest, encouraging the Burmese people and their international supporters to persevere in their struggle: "This is not yet the end—we have a long way to go, and the way might be very, very hard, so please stand by."[3] What lasts, what "you can't leave behind," are things like taking up one's cross and following Jesus by identifying with the oppressed—and the similarly cruciform practice of working for the unity of the church, which in the midst of the present disunity of the church "has to be believed to be seen."

LONGING FOR WHAT COMES LAST—
WHAT WE'RE LOOKING FOR

"Yearning" is a word that comes to mind when trying to come up with language for describing the sound of a U2 song. Their music yearns for things to be other than they are, to be more like what comes last, without giving up hope that the status quo can be transformed in the here-and-now

3. U2, "Walk On—International Version," directed by Jonas Akerlund and produced by Nicola Doring, *U2 18 Videos*. DVD. Universal Island Records, 2006.

through participation in what lasts. It looks "for something other" ("Lemon," *Zooropa*, 1993), it yearns to be taken "to that other place" ("Beautiful Day," *All That You Can't Leave Behind*, 2000), it wants "to reach out and touch the flame/ Where the streets have no name" ("Where the Streets Have No Name," *The Joshua Tree*, 1987), but with the notable exception of their recent between-albums single "Window in the Skies" (*U218 Singles*, 2006) it stops short of reveling in the fulfillment of that for which it yearns. It's not unlike the concept that the ancient Christian mystics had of the ceaseless stretching forth of the soul toward God, the desire for God that is never fully satisfied in this life but always seeks deeper and deeper levels of intimacy with the divine. This understanding of Christian spirituality was rooted in Scripture, for the noun some of the Greek church fathers employed to name this concept, *epektasis*, is derived from the corresponding verb that Paul uses as a participle in Phil 3:13–14 to describe our active relationship to the not-yet-realized dimension of the Christian life: "Beloved, I do not consider that I have made it my own; but this one thing I do: forgetting what lies behind and straining forward (*epektei-nomenos*) to what lies ahead, I press on toward the goal for the prize of the heavenly call of God in Christ Jesus."[4]

The band's most successful single ever is one of those yearning songs. "With or Without You" from *The Joshua Tree*

4. Both the noun *epektasis* and the verb *epekteinō* are employed in the expression of this understanding of Christian spirituality throughout the homilies on the Song of Songs by Gregory of Nyssa (d. ca. AD 395) in particular the homilies numbered 1, 4, 6, 8, 9, 12, and 15 (Gregory of Nyssa, *Commentary on the Song of Songs*, trans. Casimir McCambley [Archbishop Iakovos Library of Ecclesiastical and Historical Sources, no. 12; Brookline, MA: Hellenic College Press, 1987] 54, 99, 127–28, 161, 183, 217, 223, 265).

(1987) gives voice to the yearning for a difficult relationship to be other than it is. (It makes me feel really old to realize that when "With or Without You" was in heavy radio rotation late in the spring of my freshman year in college, many college undergraduate readers of this book weren't even born!) Various non-lyrical aspects of the song evoke yearning: The Edge's ethereal, whistle-like infinite sustain guitar notes; Adam's relentlessly pulsating bass line; the pleading wail of Bono's voice in the final chorus; and Larry's drumming that in the studio album version seems to pick up steam in the final few bars and drive toward something beyond the song, even as The Edge in minimalist fashion resists a grand finish and everything else is winding down and fading away.

THE ELUSIVE MUSE AND THE ESCHATOLOGY OF RELATIONSHIP

Bono wrote "With or Without You" during a period when he was torn between artistic creativity and the responsibilities of family life, and he felt he was losing his creative muse—"on a bed of nails she makes me wait." But like all U2 songs, no one explanation, not even the original inspiration of a song, can exhaust the song's multiple layers of meaning. At one level it can be taken as a song about the pain of fallen relationships and about responding in a Christlike manner when the other hurts us—"And you give/And you give/And you give yourself away." At another level the song can be heard in light of broken ecclesial relationships. Bono didn't have the quest for Christian unity in the midst of the church's current divisions in mind when he wrote the song, but that application doesn't do violence to the way it explores the eschatology of interpersonal relationships.

"With or Without You" takes a cliché—"can't live with 'em, can't live without 'em"—and turns it into a truth about the contradictions of relationships. We often find it impossible to live with the other, and yet the truth is that we can't live without the other, because the other belongs to our very identity as persons-in-relationship. That's true of human relationships in general, and it's true of relationships within the body of Christ in particular. Because we're one body, because we're members of one another, we can't live without another member of the body of Christ.

Yet in the midst of the current divisions of the church, we find it all too easy to decide that we can't live with certain other Christians—that it would be easier simply to live without them. We tend to explain denominational identity in terms of how our denomination isn't like other denominations. We pride ourselves in the superiority of our own denomination and contend that we have no need to seek full visible unity with other churches from which we're separated, for we don't think we need them—we're doing quite well on our own, thank you very much, and at any rate visible unity with other traditions would compromise our distinctiveness. So we're tempted to think. But we can't live without those from whom we are separated in the divided body of Christ. The body of Christ is wounded, and some of those wounds were inflicted by other churches on our own communion long, long ago, while other wounds have been inflicted more recently by fellow members of our own denominations in the intra-denominational strife that has torn apart most Christian communions today. It would be so easy simply to go our separate ways and live without them, but in light of Jesus's prayer for the visible unity of his followers, we can't live without them. The appropriate response to the fellow Christians we believe are responsible for our wounds is Jesus's response to those who wounded him: "And you give yourself away."

Seeking unity with other Christians requires some self-sacrifice. It also requires an appropriate eschatological perspective. We will one day live with one another when we gather around the table of the messianic banquet (Isa 25:6–8, Matt 22:1–14, Luke 13:29 and 14:7–24, Rev 19:9). That banquet is already a present reality, for the church is one body of Christ and whenever we gather around the Lord's table, we're participating in a unity that will one day be fully realized when we all share the heavenly realities of the body and blood of the risen Christ face-to-face. But we don't yet live with one another with a unity sufficiently visible for the world to notice. The not-yet-realized nature of Christian unity motivates us to seek visible unity in the present.

STRIVING AFTER THE HOPE OF UNITY

This tension between the already and the not yet of Christian unity can be illustrated by aspects of other performances of "With or Without You" beyond the album version. In our car is a mix CD with five different versions of "With or Without You," which is one of my wife's favorite U2 songs and which our toddler-age son enjoyed hearing ad infinitum while strapped into his car seat—until he more recently decided that there were other songs he wanted to hear over and over again. We used to call it his "driving song." One of those versions is the audio from the Tempe, Arizona, Joshua Tree Tour concert at Sun Devil Stadium in December 1987 featured in the *Rattle and Hum* film—in my opinion, the best live performance of the song ever recorded.[5] In that performance, an extended 20-bar bridge after the final chorus features a guitar solo in which The Edge moves sonically closer and closer to realizing what the music seeks and just about gets there when it leads into a new coda with Bono singing, "Yeah—we'll shine like stars in the summer night, we'll shine like stars in the winter night; one heart, one hope, one love." "Shine like stars"—does that sound familiar? It echoes Phil 2:14–15: "Do all things without murmuring and complaining, so that you may be blameless and innocent, children of God without blemish in the midst of a crooked and perverse generation, in which you shine like stars in the world." The added coda makes the things hoped for in the song more explicit, but it keeps them in the future. Thus Bono follows up this burst of hopeful exultation by singing once more about the present, "With or without you/I can't live with or without you," and the stretching forth of The Edge's guitar toward the day when we will shine like stars and we will truly have one heart, one hope, and one love must continue, since it hasn't quite made it there yet.

The quest for Christian unity has made amazing progress in the last century. When the modern ecumenical movement had its public beginning at the World Missionary Conference in Edinburgh, Scotland, in 1910, those who attended could scarcely have anticipated the breakthroughs in Catholic-Protestant relations, for example, that emerged in the second half of the twentieth century. We have good reason to hope confidently that the body of Christ will shine like stars in a dark world and that we will one day display to

5. U2, *Rattle and Hum*. DVD. Directed by Phil Joanou. Paramount, 1988 (DVD release, 1999).

the world one heart, one hope, one love—but it must remain a hope. That means resisting the temptation to be content with how things are in relations between our churches, no matter how much progress we might have made. Like The Edge's guitar solo in Sun Devil Stadium, we strive after what we hope for, and sometimes we draw close to realizing that hope, yet still we await the surprising work of the Spirit that will make us one. Meanwhile, we keep striving.

RESISTING RESIGNATION TO THE STATUS QUO

Another version on that CD is from a concert in Sydney, Australia, during the "Zoomerang" leg of the ZooTV Tour in November 1993.[6] To say that this is a very different rendition of the song is an understatement. This performance fully lives into the dark side of this song. If the Joshua Tree Tour performance accentuated the hope that the relationship might yet be healed, this ZooTV performance gives in to despairing rage at what's gone wrong with the relationship. The once ethereal infinite sustain notes from The Edge's guitar are now discordant feedback. Adam's once mesmerizing bass line is now a driving monotony. Larry, whose accented back beats previously gave even this song about relational difficulty something approaching a romantic air, is now hammering away with oddly syncopated, almost out-of-kilter thuds on his tom-toms, making the song seem to stagger on its feet. Most significantly, Bono is dressed as the devil. Taking a cue from C. S. Lewis' *Screwtape Letters*,[7] Bono is in character as Mr. McPhisto, a sort of Irish parallel to

6. U2, *Zoo TV, Live from Sydney*. DVD. Island, 1994 (DVD release, 2006).

7. C. S. Lewis, *The Screwtape Letters* (New York: Macmillan, 1943).

the character Mephistopheles in the Germanic legend that inspired Goethe's *Faust*, but played by an aging, washed-up pop star. Now the devil himself, whose Greek name *diabolos* in the New Testament means "divider," sings of the relational division he instigates. Bono's voice, channeling the McPhisto persona, embodies jaded resignation.

Despite all the progress of the past century, the future of the ecumenical movement is now very much in doubt. As this book has already mentioned more than once, ecumenism has experienced numerous setbacks in the last few years. In many ways the church is becoming more rather than less divided, and if we care deeply about ecumenism, there are days when the widespread lack of interest in the quest for visible Christian unity dashes our hopes and makes us feel just about like the mood captured by the Sydney performance of "With or Without You." The temptation is to resign ourselves to the way things are and content ourselves with the separated existence of our churches. But when we find ourselves yielding to pessimism about the possibility that we might somehow overcome our divisions, we should remember that the source of such thinking is the diabolical one, the one who divides.

BAPTIZED INTO DIVISION

Still another very different version of "With or Without You" isn't actually performed by U2. It's a haunting choral arrangement by the Kolancy Brothers sung by the Belgian girls' choir Scala with piano accompaniment.[8] Beth Maynard, an Episcopal priest who co-edited *Get Up Off*

8. Scala & Kolancy Brothers, *Dream On* (Play It Again Sam UK, 2003) [CD].

Your Knees: Preaching the U2 Catalog[9] and who maintains the U2Sermons blog, observed that hearing these innocent young voices sing this song about the pain of adult relationships "leaves me feeling sort of like I do when a child reads the role of Pilate, or Peter's betrayal, in the Passion on Palm Sunday."[10]

Just as children aren't spared the consequences of the dysfunctional relationships of their parents, so it is with those who are nurtured toward faith and come to embrace the faith within the divided church. When we're baptized, we're baptized into the one body of Christ—that's the "already" of our baptism and its connection with the church. But there's also a "not yet" dimension to our baptisms, in that we're also baptized into the church's divisions. The churches of our baptisms do belong to the one universal church, but these churches are also divided from other churches that belong to the universal church—thus the paradox of being baptized into the one church and into its divisions. Like children who inescapably inherit the world of broken relationships simply because they're born into it, every Christian is reborn into a church that is sinfully divided. That means the quest for Christian unity isn't optional—it's the obligation of every baptized believer.

CRYING OUT FOR UNITY

So what can ordinary baptized believers do about a quest that has tended to be a high-level pursuit by theologians, profes-

9. Raewynne J. Whiteley and Beth Maynard, eds., *Get Up Off Your Knees: Preaching the U2 Catalog* (Cambridge, MA: Cowley, 2003).

10. Beth Maynard, "U2Sermons—Blog for the Book 'Get Up Off Your Knees: Preaching the U2 Catalog," March 31, 2006. Online: http://u2sermons.blogspot.com/2006/03/you-give-yourself-away.html.

sional ecumenists, and denominational leaders? In chapter 4, I suggested ten things all Christians can do for the unity of the church. The most important of those was the practice of praying for Christian unity. As chapter 4 observed, if unity is ultimately the gift of God, and if it comes about when and how Christ wills through the ever-surprising work of the Spirit, then the most significant thing we can do for the unity of the church is to ask God to make it so among us. This belongs to what ecumenists call "spiritual ecumenism," which begins with the recognition of the spiritual unity that otherwise divided believers already share in Christ and in the Spirit.[11] The spiritual ecumenism embodied in praying for unity is the expression of the quest for Christian unity upon which all other ecumenical endeavors depend, and it's something that all Christians can practice.

Joining Jesus in praying for the unity of his church embodies the eschatology of ecumenism. It recognizes and seeks to do something about the not-yet dimension of Christian unity. To pray for unity is to confess that we do not presently have the unity Christ wants his church to have. To pray for unity is to ask, "Is it I, Lord?"—that is, to confess that we've contributed to the church's disunity through our own divisiveness and through our own failures to seek what Christ seeks for his church.

Like "With or Without You," the song "One" took on a life of its own in live performances. During the ZooTV tour Bono started adding this coda: "Hear us coming, Lord/Hear us call/hear us knocking, we're knocking at your door." In the context of the song, that coda was a prayer for oneness—a

11. Walter Cardinal Kasper, *A Handbook of Spiritual Ecumenism* (Hyde Park, NY: New City, 2007).

prayer for the reconciliation of a relationship at the breaking point. It doesn't take too much imagination to hear this coda in a different light as a prayer for Christian unity that follows in the footsteps of Jesus's prayer for the unity of his church in John 17. Such prayer has all Christians as the beneficiaries of its intercession and invites all Christians to join in its voicing and its fulfillment, for ecumenism means you, too. It is as much a universal obligation of the Christian life as the Great Commission to "Go therefore and make disciples of all nations, baptizing them in the name of the Father and of the Son and of the Holy Spirit, and teaching them to obey everything that I have commanded you" (Matt 28:19–20). The promise given to those who heed that commission also applies to those who take up the quest for Christian unity: "And remember, I am with you always, to the end of the age" (Matt 28:20). That, too, belongs to the eschatology of ecumenism.

I conclude this book by inviting you to join me, and Christ and all of his body, in praying that the unity of the church might soon be manifested on earth, as it is in heaven. *Heavenly Father, who infinitely more passionately than our earthly mothers and fathers longs for your children to live harmoniously with one another as members of one close family: grant your church the oneness that belongs to you and your Son, through Jesus Christ our Lord, who lives and reigns with you in the unity of the Holy Spirit, one God, now and forever. Hear us call, and help us to heed your call to maintain the unity of your church. Amen.*

Appendix A

Resources for Ecumenical Engagement

THIS ANNOTATED BIBLIOGRAPHY POINTS readers of *Ecumenism Means You, Too* to selected key resources for learning more about the ecumenical movement and becoming actively involved in its advance. More comprehensive bibliographical guides are listed under the first subsection below. An excellent place to begin is the *Introduction to Ecumenism* by Jeffrey Gros, Eamon McManus, and Ann Riggs. One might then study any agreed texts and reports that have resulted from international dialogues between one's own denominational tradition and other churches before exploring some of the other resources listed here.

ECUMENICAL BIBLIOGRAPHICAL RESOURCES

Centro Pro Unione Bulletin. Online: http://www.prounione.urbe.it/att-act/e_bulletin_fr.html.

> One issue each year of this semi-annual periodical published by the Centro Pro Unione in Rome (see under Ecumenical Institutions and Organizations below) includes the section "A Bibliography of Interchurch and Interconfessional Dialogues."

Crow, Paul A. *The Ecumenical Movement in Bibliographical Outline*. New York: Department of Faith and Order, National Council of the Churches of Christ in the USA, 1965.

A now-dated bibliography, but useful for identifying key resources from the early decades of the
modern ecumenical movement.

Fahey, Michael A. *Ecumenism: A Bibliographical Overview.* Bibliographies
and Indexes in Religious Studies, no. 23. Westport, CT: Greenwood,
1992.

An annotated bibliography that includes entries for
over 1,300 books on ecumenism published between
1950 and 1992 and describes 85 journals devoted
to ecumenism. The annotations offer a thorough
analysis of the strengths and weaknesses of specific
publications. The volume provides a theological and
historical record of Orthodox, Catholic, Anglican,
and Protestant ecumenical literature, and serves as
a guide to works on the World Council of Churches,
the Second Vatican Council, and modern bilateral
dialogues.

Prairie Centre for Ecumenism. "Bibliography of Ecumenism and the
Ecumenical Movement." Online: http://www.ecumenism.net/docu/
bibliography_w-z.htm.

A bibliography compiled automatically from da-
tabase searches of university library catalogs, ar-
ranged alphabetically by author. Maintained by an
ecumenical institute sponsored by seven denominations in Saskatoon, Saskatchewan, Canada.

United States Conference of Catholic Bishops. "A Selected Bibliography."
Online: http://www.usccb.org/seia/publications.htm.

A select online bibliography maintained by the
USCCB Bishops' Committee for Ecumenical and
Interreligious Affairs. Texts listed in the bibliography that are available elsewhere online are
hyperlinked.

INTRODUCTIONS TO ECUMENISM, HISTORICAL SURVEYS, AND REFERENCE WORKS

Faith and Order Commission of the World Council of Churches. *Towards Sharing the One Faith: A Study Guide for Discussion Groups.* Geneva: WCC, 1996.

> A useful group study guide intended to help ecumenical and denominational groups enter into the process of exploring the faith of the church and of recognizing this faith in their own lives and the lives of other Christian communities, in the hope that such study will move Christians toward common witness to the faith in liturgy and life and toward growth together in visible unity.

Gassmann, Günther. "What Is Faith and Order?" Online: http://www .oikoumene.org/en/resources/documents/wcc-commissions/faith-and-order-commission/xii-essays/11–08–95-what-is-faith-and-order-guenther-gassmann.html.

> An immensely informative introduction to the theological heart of the modern ecumenical movement, prepared by a former director of the World Council of Churches Faith and Order Commission for a Faith and Order consultation with Younger Theologians held at Turku, Finland, August 3–11, 1995.

Gros, Jeffrey, Eamon McManus, and Ann Riggs. *Introduction to Ecumenism.* New York: Paulist, 1998.

> An accessible introduction to the history, biblical and theological basis, and institutional expressions of the modern ecumenical movement. Though written primarily from a Roman Catholic perspective, the book provides an excellent basic ecumenical orientation for all Christians. This text is an excel-

lent starting place for readers who want to learn more about ecumenism.

Hjelm, Norman A., editor. *Faith and Order: Toward a North American Conference. Study Guide.* Grand Rapids: Eerdmans, 2005.

This small book (50 pages) provides a fine introduction to the Faith and Order stream of the ecumenical movement, which is really the movement's indispensable theological heart. This study guide was conceived to introduce North American Christians to the importance of Faith and Order ecumenism in preparation for a major Conference on Faith and Order in North America in connection with the fiftieth anniversary of the landmark 1957 Oberlin, Ohio, conference on "The Nature of the Unity We Seek." While the envisioned conference was ultimately not held, this book continues to serve as a useful introduction to an increasingly neglected dimension of ecumenism. It is notable for its attention to the concerns of evangelical and Pentecostal communions that have not historically been involved in Faith and Order ecumenism.

Kasper, Walter Cardinal. "Nature and Purpose of Ecumenical Dialogue." Online: http://www.vatican.va/roman_curia/pontifical_councils/ chrstuni/card-kasper-docs/rc_pc_chrstuni_doc_20030227_ ecumenical-dialogue_en.html.

A helpful introduction to the nature and purpose of ecumenical dialogue in Roman Catholic perspective from the president of the Pontifical Council for Promoting Christian unity, who offers a candid overview of the evolution of the Catholic stance toward the modern ecumenical movement from outright opposition at its beginning to irrevocable commitment to it at the Second Vatican Council and thereafter.

Lossky, Nicholas, editor. *Dictionary of the Ecumenical Movement*. 2nd ed. Geneva: WCC, 2002.

> A helpful reference work for those seeking to learn more about ecumenism, this dictionary features entries on all aspects of the ecumenical movement as well as the churches that belong to the divisions of the one church, written by internationally recognized ecumenists and experts on each Christian denomination/communion.

Meyer, Harding. *That All May Be One: Perceptions and Models of Ecumenicity*. Translated by William G. Rusch. Grand Rapids: Eerdmans, 1999.

> A more technical survey of the diverse theoretical approaches behind the practice of ecumenical encounter throughout the history of the ecumenical movement. This book provides detailed explanations of terms and categories that have become commonplace in ecumenical discussions, such as "differentiated consensus" and "unity in reconciled diversity."

National Council of the Churches of Christ in the USA. *Faith and Order Commission Handbook*. New York: NCCCUSA Faith and Order Office, 2008. Online: http://www.ncccusa.org/pdfs/FOhandbook2008.pdf.

> This handbook is intended not only to orient new members of the Faith and Order Commission of the National Council of the Churches of Christ in the USA to the work of the Commission, but also to introduce other interested persons to Faith and Order ecumenism. Available online as a PDF file, it includes a concise history of the Faith and Order movement and an explanation of ecumenical methodology by noted American ecumenists, as well as

a compilation of quotations from key ecumenical documents and a "Beginner's Bibliography."

Rusch, William G. *Ecumenical Reception: Its Challenge and Opportunity*. Grand Rapids: Eerdmans, 2007.

An introduction to the processes by which the churches respond to the steps toward unity represented by the agreements reached in ecumenical dialogues.

World Council of Churches. *A History of the Ecumenical Movement*. 3 vols. Edited by Ruth Rouse, Stephen Neill, Harold Edward Fey, John H. Y. Briggs, Mercy Amba Oduyoye, and Georgios Tsetses. Geneva: WCC, 2004.

The definitive historical account of the ecumenical movement, covering developments from 1517 to 2000.

ECUMENICAL INSTITUTIONS AND ORGANIZATIONS

Center for Catholic and Evangelical Theology. Online: http://www.e-ccet .org.

The Center for Catholic and Evangelical Theology is an ecumenical organization that seeks to cultivate faithfulness to the gospel of Jesus Christ throughout the churches by nurturing theology that is catholic and evangelical, obedient to Holy Scripture and committed to the dogmatic, liturgical, ethical, and institutional continuity of the church. The Center challenges the churches to claim their identity as members of the One, Holy, Catholic and Apostolic Church. It affirms the Great Tradition and seeks to stimulate fresh thinking and passion for mission. To achieve this goal the Center sponsors projects,

conferences, and publications (including the journal *Pro Ecclesia*).

Centro Pro Unione (Rome, Italy). Online: http://www.prounione.urbe.it/
home_en.html.

> Founded and directed by the Society of the
> Atonement, the Centro Pro Unione ("Center for
> Union") is an ecumenical research and action cen-
> ter. Its purpose is to give space for dialogue, and to
> be a place for study, research, and formation in ecu-
> menism: theological, pastoral, social, and spiritual.
> The Centro maintains a research library, publishes
> the *Centro Pro Unione Bulletin*, hosts lectures and
> conferences, supplies material in support of the an-
> nual Week of Prayer for Christian Unity (see below
> under "Prayer for Christian Unity"), and offers a
> graduate-level Summer Course in Ecumenism.

Christian Churches Together in the USA. Online: http://www.christian
churchestogether.org.

> Officially organized in 2006, Christian Churches
> Together is intended as a forum of ecumenical dia-
> logue and witness involving the participation of rep-
> resentatives from all five major Christian families of
> churches in the United States: Catholic, Orthodox,
> historic Protestant, evangelical/Pentecostal, and
> historic racial/ethnic. The organization seeks to
> provide a context—marked by prayer, theologi-
> cal dialogue and fellowship—in which churches
> can develop relationships with other churches
> with whom they presently have little contact, and
> it hopes to offer a significant and credible voice in
> speaking to contemporary culture on issues of life,
> social justice and peace.

Churches Uniting in Christ (CUIC). Online: http://www.cuicinfo.org.

> Churches Uniting in Christ is a relationship among ten Christian communions that have pledged to live more closely together in expressing their unity in Christ and to combat racism together. CUIC is both an outgrowth of and successor to the Consultation on Church Union (COCU), an organization that worked for more than 40 years toward the day when Christians can become more fully reconciled to each other. Member communions presently include the African Methodist Episcopal Church, the African Methodist Episcopal Zion Church, the Christian Church (Disciples of Christ), the Christian Methodist Episcopal Church, the Episcopal Church USA, the International Council of Community Churches, the Moravian Church Northern Province, the Presbyterian Church (USA), the United Church of Christ, and the United Methodist Church, with the Evangelical Lutheran Church in America having the status "Partners in Mission and Dialogue."

Graymoor Ecumenical and Interreligious Institute. Online: http://www .geii.org.

> As a ministry of the Franciscan Friars of the Atonement, the mission of the Graymoor Ecumenical and Interreligious Institute is to promote Christian unity and interreligious dialogue in North America. It seeks to fulfill this mission by engaging in study and research in the ecumenical and interreligious movements through writing, workshops, and participation in dialogues between and among the churches as well as with different faith communities at the local and national level; by offering personal expertise on ecumenical and interreligious matters, making staff available upon

request for lectures and short courses, and offering information to news media and researchers; publication of the journal *Ecumenical Trends* and publication and distribution of resource materials for the annual observance of the Week of Prayer for Christian Unity; and by co-sponsorship of the biennial Northeast Ecumenical Institute at Graymoor and faculty participation in an annual summer course which introduces students to ecumenical and interreligious movements at the Centro Pro Unione in Rome.

Institute for Ecumenical Research (Strasbourg, France). Online: http://www.ecumenical-institute.org.

Sponsored by the Lutheran World Federation, the Institute seeks to bring together scholarly research and service to the churches in three major areas of work: ecumenical research, ecumenical dialogue, and ecumenical communication and reception.

National Council of the Churches of Christ in the USA. Online: http://www.ncccusa.org.

Since its founding in 1950, the NCCCUSA has been the primary institutional structure for ecumenical cooperation among Christians in the United States. Member faith groups from a wide spectrum of Protestant, Anglican, Orthodox, Evangelical, historic African-American, and Peace churches, include approximately 45 million persons in more than 100,000 local congregations.

National Council of the Churches of Christ in the USA Faith and Order Commission. Online: http://www.ncccusa.org/about/unityhome.html.

As summarized in the constitution of the NCCC-USA, the mission of its Faith and Order Commission is to "affirm the oneness of the Church of Jesus

Christ and keep before the churches the Gospel call
to visible unity in one faith and one Eucharist communion, expressed in worship and in common life
in Christ, in order that the world may believe." The
Commission sponsors annual study groups, a series
of books and occasional papers, and the electronic
journal *New Horizons in Faith and Order*.

North American Academy of Ecumenists. Online: https://www.naae.net.

Founded in 1957, The North American Academy of
Ecumenists is a scholarly and professional community of those actively involved in making the unity
of Christ's church visible through their teaching,
research, ecclesiastic work, and common witness.
The goal of the NAAE is to inform, relate, and
encourage men and women whose profession or
ministry in the church involves them in ecumenical activities and studies. It understands its unique
contribution to be providing ecumenists with an
open structure for exploring issues too important
to be left exclusively to official ecumenical agencies
and projects. The NAAE holds annual conferences,
is affiliated with the *Journal of Ecumenical Studies*,
and publishes an occasional newsletter, *NAAE Links*
(available online in PDF format).

Pontifical Council for Promoting Christian Unity. Online: http://www
.vatican.va/roman_curia/pontifical_councils/chrstuni/documents/
rc_pc_chrstuni_pro_20051996_chrstuni_pro_en.html.

Established in 1960 by Pope John XXIII, conve-
ner of the Second Vatican Council, the PCPCU is
entrusted with the promotion within the Catholic
Church of an authentic ecumenical spirit according to the conciliar decree *Unitatis redintegratio*
and aims to develop dialogue and collaboration
with the other churches and world communions.

Since its creation, it has also established a cordial cooperation with the World Council of Churches and regularly names Catholic observers at various ecumenical gatherings and invites observers or "fraternal delegates" of other churches or ecclesial communities to major events of the Catholic Church. The PCPCU publishes a journal called *Information Service* four times a year, in English and French.

World Council of Churches. Online: http://www.oikoumene.org.

The WCC is the broadest and most inclusive among the many organized expressions of the modern ecumenical movement. It brings together 349 churches, denominations and church fellowships in more than 110 countries and territories throughout the world, representing over 560 million Christians and including most of the world's Orthodox churches, scores of Anglican, Baptist, Lutheran, Methodist and Reformed churches, as well as many United and Independent churches. While the bulk of the WCC's founding churches were European and North American, today most member churches are in Africa, Asia, the Caribbean, Latin America, the Middle East and the Pacific. It describes itself as a fellowship of churches which confess the Lord Jesus Christ as God and Savior according to the Scriptures and therefore seek to fulfill together their common calling to the glory of the one God, Father, Son and Holy Spirit, with the goal of visible unity in one faith and one Eucharistic fellowship, expressed in worship and in common life in Christ.

World Council of Churches Faith and Order Commission. Online: http://www.oikoumene.org/en/who-are-we/organization-structure/consultative-bodies/faith-and-order.html.

The Faith and Order Commission has an aim integral to the work of the WCC: "to proclaim the oneness of the church of Jesus Christ and to call the churches to the goal of visible unity." The chief means of achieving this goal is through study programs dealing with theological questions that divide the churches. The Faith and Order plenary commission has 120 members—pastors, laypersons, academics, and church leaders from around the world—each nominated by his or her church. The Faith and Order Commission includes the full membership and participation of several other churches who are not members of the WCC, among them the Roman Catholic Church. Thirty members of this Commission constitute the Faith and Order standing commission, who meet at least every 18 months and guide the study programs of Faith and Order.

ECUMENICAL PERIODICALS

Centro Pro Unione Bulletin. Online: http://www.prounione.urbe.it/att-act/e_bulletin_fr.html.

A semi-annual journal published in English by the Centro Pro Unione in Rome. One of the issues each year contains a multilingual bibliography of interchurch and interconfessional dialogues.

The Ecumenical Review. Online: http://www.wiley.com/bw/journal.asp?ref=0013-0796&site=1.

A quarterly ecumenical theological journal published by the World Council of Churches. Each issue focuses on a theme of current importance to the movement for Christian unity, and each volume includes academic as well as practical analysis of significant moments in the quest for closer church fellowship and interreligious dialogue.

Ecumenical Trends. Online: http://www.geii.org/ecumenical_trends.htm.

Published by the Franciscan Friars of the Atonement at the Graymoor Ecumenical and Interreligious Institute, *Ecumenical Trends* is a monthly (except August) journal that publishes articles on the ecumenical and interreligious movements. *Ecumenical Trends* reports on current trends and progress in these movements around the world. It covers theological consultations, conversations, dialogues and cooperation, and it notes the availability of documents and resources and occasionally publishes the text of dialogue documents.

Journal of Ecumenical Studies. Online: http://journal.jesdialogue.org.

A quarterly ecumenical journal published by the Dialogue Institute at Temple University in Philadelphia in association with the North American Academy of Ecumenists. Gives attention to interreligious dialogue as well as ecumenism proper.

Pro Ecclesia: A Journal of Catholic and Evangelical Theology. Online: http://www.e-ccet.org/pe.htm.

Published by the Center for Catholic and Evangelical Theology, *Pro Ecclesia* seeks to give contemporary expression to the one apostolic faith and its classic traditions, working for and manifesting the church's unity by research, theological construction, and free exchange of opinion. Members of its advisory council represent communities committed to the authority of Holy Scripture, ecumenical dogmatic teaching and the structural continuity of the church, and are themselves dedicated to maintaining and invigorating these commitments. The

journal publishes biblical, liturgical, historical
and doctrinal articles that promote or illumine its
purposes.

AGREED TEXTS AND REPORTS FROM BILATERAL
AND MULTILATERAL DIALOGUES

Burgess, Joseph A., and Jeffrey Gros, editors. *Building Unity: Ecumenical
   Dialogues with Roman Catholic Participation in the United States.*
   New York: Paulist, 1989.

   The most complete compendium of ecumenical
   documents produced in the United States including
   conciliar and bilateral dialogues in which Roman
   Catholics have participated.

Burgess, Joseph A., and Jeffrey Gros, editors. *Growing Consensus: Church
   Dialogues in the United States, 1962–1991.* New York: Paulist, 1995.

   Includes ecumenical documents produced by bilateral, multilateral, and church union dialogues in the
   United States.

Centro Pro Unione. "Interconfessional Dialogues." Online: http://www
   .prounione.urbe.it/dia-int/e_dialogues.html.

   This web page maintained by the Centro Pro Unione
   provides links to online agreed texts from selected
   interconfessional dialogues. Texts from dialogues
   involving the following communions and organizations are currently linked: Anglican Consultative
   Council, Roman Catholic Church, Assyrian
   Church of the East, Baptist World Alliance, Coptic
   Orthodox, Mlankara Syrian Orthodox, Disciples of
   Christ, World Evangelical Alliance, World Alliance
   of Reformed Churches, World Council of Church
   Joint Working Group, Lutheran World Federation,

Mennonite World Conference, World Methodist Council, Pentecostals, and the Orthodox Church.

Gassmann, Günther, editor. *Documentary History of Faith and Order 1963–1993*. Geneva: WCC, 1993.

> The three decades between the fourth and fifth world conferences on Faith and Order (Montreal 1963 and Santiago de Compostela 1993) were a period of important and creative work by the WCC's Commission on Faith and Order. While continuing and deepening ecumenical theological discussions that date back to the first world conference in 1927, several major studies have significantly advanced the search for the visible unity of the church. At the same time, the constituency of Faith and Order broadened, particularly through the full participation in the commission of the Roman Catholic Church. The editor of this book introduces the texts, setting them in their historical context and linking them together.

Kinnamon, Michael, and Brian Cope, editors. *The Ecumenical Movement: An Anthology of Key Texts and Voices*. Grand Rapids: Eerdmans, 1997.

> Included in this exhaustive collection of documents from the twentieth-century ecumenical movement are significant passages from the most widely influential texts produced by assemblies, conferences, and studies of the World Council of Churches and similar bodies, covering the three broad areas of historic concern within modern ecumenism: faith and order, life and work, and mission and evangelism.

Lutheran World Federation and Roman Catholic Church. *Joint Declaration on the Doctrine of Justification*. Grand Rapids: Eerdmans, 2000. Online: http://www.vatican.va/roman_curia/pontifical_councils/

chrstuni/documents/rc_pc_chrstuni_doc_31101999_cath-luth-joint-declaration_en.html.

Wainwright, Geoffrey. "World Methodist Council and the Joint Declaration on the Doctrine of Justification." *Pro Ecclesia* 16, no. 1(2007) 7–13. Online: http://www.vatican.va/roman_curia/pontifical_councils/chrstuni/meth-council-docs/rc_pc_chrstuni_doc_20060723_text-association_en.html.

> The *JDDJ* was officially confirmed by the Lutheran World Federation and the Roman Catholic Church on October 31, 1999, in Augsburg, Germany—482 years after Martin Luther posted the "95 Theses" on the door of the *Schlosskirche* in Wittenburg. This "differentiated consensus" on the doctrine that divided the Western church in the sixteenth century was the outcome of decades of dialogue between representatives of the Lutheran and Catholic churches and is one of the most significant recent achievements of the ecumenical movement. In 2006 the *JDDJ* was officially joined by the World Methodist Council, so that it may now be said that there is substantial agreement between Catholics, Lutherans, and Methodists in their teaching about justification by faith as the gracious gift of God. Along with *Baptism, Eucharist and Ministry* (World Council of Churches), the *JDDJ* is one of the two most significant advances attained in ecumenical dialogue thus far.

Prairie Centre for Ecumenism. "Ecumenical Dialogues." Online: http://www.ecumenism.net/docu/dialogue.htm.

> An annotated online bibliography of many of the international and Canadian national dialogues, with most of the reports and agreed texts hyperlinked to online sources. Maintained by an ecumenical

institute sponsored by seven denominations in Saskatoon, Saskatchewan, Canada.

Rusch, William G., and Jeffrey Gros, editors. *Deepening Communion: International Ecumenical Documents with Roman Catholic Participation.* Washington, DC: United States Catholic Conference, 1998.

A collection of twenty agreed texts that represent the fruit of international ecumenical dialogue between the Roman Catholic Church and the Lutheran World Federation, the World Alliance of Reformed Churches, the World Methodist Council, the Christian Church (Disciples of Christ), the Baptist World Alliance, representatives of the worldwide Pentecostal movement, representatives of the worldwide Evangelical movement, and the Joint Working Group of the World Council of Churches during the period 1972 to 1996.

Veliko, Lydia, and Jeffrey Gros, editors. *Growing Consensus II.* Washington, DC: United States Catholic Conference, 2004.

A comprehensive collection of the major American ecumenical documents between 1992 and 2004. Among churches included are Catholic, historic Protestant, Orthodox, Anabaptist, and Evangelical.

Vischer, Lukas, editor. *A Documentary History of the Faith and Order Movement 1927–1963.* St. Louis: Bethany, 1963.

A collection of key texts that document the rise of the Faith and Order stream of the modern ecumenical movement from the initial international conference on Faith and Order to the early years of the movement's coming of age in the 1960s.

World Council of Churches. *Baptism, Eucharist and Ministry.* Faith and Order Paper no. 111. Geneva: WCC, 1982. Online: http://www.oikoumene.org/fileadmin/files/wcc-main/documents/p2/FO1982_111_en.pdf.

BEM is the product of a fifty-year process of ecumenical study and consultation sponsored by the Faith and Order Commission of the World Council of Churches addressing the three most significant ecclesiological barriers to full communion between the churches. The text was recommended unanimously by over 100 theologians representing virtually all major church traditions at a plenary meeting of the WCC Faith and Order Commission in Lima, Peru in 1982. Along with the *Joint Declaration on the Doctrine of Justification* (Roman Catholic Church, Lutheran World Federation, and World Methodist Council), *BEM* is one of the two most significant advances attained in ecumenical dialogue thus far and is easily the most widely distributed and studied of all ecumenical documents. It has served as the basis for several "mutual recognition" agreements between communions.

World Council of Churches. *Growth in Agreement.* 3 vols. Vol. 1, *Growth in Agreement: Reports and Agreed Statements of Ecumenical Conversations on a World Level.* Edited by Harding Meyer and Lukas Vischer. Faith and Order Paper, no. 108. Geneva: WCC, 1984.

World Council of Churches. *Growth in Agreement II: Reports and Agreed Statements of Ecumenical Conversations on a World Level, 1982–1998.* Edited by Jeffrey Gros, Harding Meyer, and William G. Rusch. Geneva: WCC, 2000.

World Council of Churches. *Growth in Agreement III: International Dialogue Texts and Agreed Statements, 1998–2005.* Edited by Jeffrey Gros, Thomas F. Best, and Lorelei F. Fuchs. Geneva: WCC, 2007.

The definitive print collection of reports and agreed statements from bilateral and multilateral dialogues adopted from 1971 through the present. The *Growth in Agreement* series provides an excellent

set of resources for individual, group, and congre-
gational study.

PRAYER FOR CHRISTIAN UNITY

Clifford, Catherine E., editor. *A Century of Prayer for Christian Unity*.
   Grand Rapids: Eerdmans, 2009.

> This book is a celebration of the one-hundred-year
> history of the Week of Prayer for Christian Unity
> and serves as a resource for understanding the
> theology and practice of common prayer for the
> reconciliation of the churches. Contributors to this
> volume represent a cross-section of perspectives
> both denominationally including Anglican, Roman
> Catholic, Baptist, and Reformed as well as in light of
> their lived experience of Christian spirituality and
> prayer. Each essayist offers significant insights into
> the history, theology, and spirituality of the Week
> of Prayer in particular, and of ecumenical prayer
> in general.

McCullum, Hugh, and Terry MacArthur. *In God's Hands: Common Prayer
   for the World*. Rev. ed. Geneva: WCC, 2006.

> *In God's Hands* offers aids for ecumenical interces-
> sory prayer, prayer on behalf of and in solidarity
> with others. This book includes prayers and other
> worship material from many Christian traditions
> and communities. It enables the reader to jour-
> ney in prayer through each week of the year and
> through all the regions and countries of the world,
> in the hope that knowing something of these na-
> tions' and peoples' local situations, possibilities, and
> challenges will help Christians to pray for others in
> an informed way.

World Council of Churches. "In God's Hands: The Ecumenical Prayer
    Cycle." Online: http://www.oikoumene.org/en/resources/prayer-
    cycle.html.

> Each week this web page maintained by the WCC
> provides information, guidance for offering inter-
> cessory prayer, and suggested prayers for a specific
> region of the world as an expression of solidarity
> with other Christians living in that place. Many of
> the resources provided here are based on *In God's
> Hands: Common Prayer for the World* by Hugh
> McCullum and Terry MacArthur.

ASSESSMENTS OF ECUMENISM
AND PROPOSALS FOR ITS FUTURE

Braaten, Carl E., and Robert W. Jenson, editors. *In One Body Through
    the Cross: The Princeton Proposal for Christian Unity. A Call to
    the Churches from an Ecumenical Study Group.* Grand Rapids:
    Eerdmans, 2003.

> This proposal was drafted by a group of sixteen
> theologians and ecumenists from various Christian
> traditions (but not officially representing them) who
> were commissioned for this task by an independent
> ecumenical foundation, the Center for Catholic
> and Evangelical Theology. This perceptive analysis
> of the current ecumenical impasse proposes a way
> forward through a recovery of the chief historic
> goal of the modern ecumenical movement—the
> visible unity of Christians worldwide in worship,
> Eucharistic fellowship, doctrine, and witness.

Braaten, Carl E., and Robert W. Jenson, editors. *The Ecumenical Future:
    Background Papers for In One Body Through the Cross: The Princeton
    Proposal for Christian Unity.* Grand Rapids: Eerdmans, 2004.

A collection of essays by members of the working group that drafted the Princeton Proposal for Christian Unity addressing themes integral to that proposal.

Colson, Charles W., and Richard John Neuhaus, editors. *Evangelicals and Catholics Together: Toward a Common Mission.* Dallas: Word, 1995.

————. "The Gift of Salvation: A Statement of Evangelicals and Catholics Together," *First Things* (January 1998). Online: http://www.firstthings.com/article.php3?id_article=3453);

————. "Your Word Is Truth: A Statement of Evangelicals and Catholics Together, " *First Things* (August/September 2002). Online: http://www.firstthings.com/article.php3?id_article=2058);

————. "The Communion of Saints: A Statement of Evangelicals and Catholics Together," *First Things* (March 2003). Online: http://www.firstthings.com/article.php3?id_article=459);

————. "The Call to Holiness: A Statement of Evangelicals and Catholics Together," *First Things* (March 2005). Online: http://www.firstthings.com/article.php3?id_article=171);

————. "That They May Have Life: A Statement of Evangelicals and Catholics Together," *First Things* (October 2006). Online: http://www.firstthings.com/article.php3?id_article=5358).

An independent working group of Catholic and evangelical scholars and church leaders who are not officially representing their churches but who meet together regularly to discuss some of the pressing social issues of the day and to publish statements of their common convictions which they propose for consideration by Christians and their churches.

George, Timothy F., editor. *Pilgrims on the Sawdust Trail: Evangelical Ecumenism and the Quest for Christian Identity.* Grand Rapids: Baker, 2004.

A collection of papers by a wide range of theologians and ecumenists with varying relationships to evangelicalism, originally presented at an academic symposium framing contemporary issues regarding evangelical identity in ecumenical perspective.

Groupe des Dombes. *For the Conversion of the Churches.* Translated by James Grieg. Geneva: WCC, 1993.

The Groupe des Dombes is an independent ecumenical discussion group of Catholic and Protestant ecumenists in France and Switzerland founded in 1937. It has no official ecclesial status, but texts drafted by the group have been influential for international Faith and Order deliberations. This text drafted by the group challenges the divided churches to recognize that their identity is grounded in a continual conversion, without which their unity can never be realized. For an introduction to the work of the Groupe des Dombes, see Clifford, Catherine E. *The Group des Dombes: A Dialogue of Conversion.* New York: Peter Lang, 2005.

Kasper, Walter Cardinal. *That They May All Be One: The Call to Unity Today.* London: Burns & Oates, 2004.

A candid yet hopeful perspective on the quest for Christian unity and its contemporary challenges by the current president of the Pontifical Council for Promoting Christian Unity.

Kinnamon, Michael. *The Vision of the Ecumenical Movement and How It Has Been Impoverished by Its Friends.* St. Louis: Chalice, 2003.

A book-length analysis of the ecumenical status quo by a veteran ecumenist who urges those who care about ecumenical advance to recover the manner in which the modern ecumenical movement historically understood the three emphases that coalesced in the formation of the World Council of Churches—unity in mission, unity in service, and unity in faith and order—as interrelated and inseparable.

Lindbeck, George. "The Unity We Seek: Setting the Agenda for Ecumenism." *Christian Century* 122:16 (2005) 28–31. Online: http://www.religion-online.org/showarticle.asp?title=3235.

An outstanding recent overview and analysis of the current ecumenical situation by a veteran ecumenical theologian.

Murray, Paul, editor. *Receptive Ecumenism and the Call to Catholic Learning: Exploring a Way for Contemporary Ecumenism.* New York: Oxford University Press, 2008.

A collection of essays advocating an approach to ecumenical engagement characterized by self-critical receptivity, in which each church or communion asks what it needs to receive from other traditions in order to become more fully the church of Jesus Christ.

Rusch, William G. "The State and Future of the Ecumenical Movement." *Pro Ecclesia* 9:1 (2000) 8–18.

This article functions as a "state of the union" address regarding the ecumenical movement and its future, by a veteran ecumenist who once served as director of the Faith and Order Commission of the National Council of the Churches of Christ in the USA.

Appendix B

Glossary of Key Ecumenical Terms

Many of the terms defined below have already been encountered and explained in the chapters of *Ecumenism Means You, Too*. Other terms included in this glossary are employed frequently in the ecumenical literature listed in Appendix 1, and a basic grasp of their meaning will facilitate the reading of many of those texts. Words preceded by an asterisk (*) in the text of the definitions are themselves defined elsewhere in this glossary.

Bilateral dialogue—Ecumenical conversations between representatives of two church/denominational communions. Some of these, such as the series of dialogues between the Methodist World Council and the Roman Catholic Church, have full *visible unity as their ultimate goal. Others, such as the conversations between the Roman Catholic Church and the Baptist World Alliance, seek rather to increase mutual understanding and to find common ways of bearing witness to the gospel and speaking to moral concerns shared by both communions.

Catholicity—From a Greek word meaning "according to the whole," catholicity as a mark of the church refers quantitatively to the universal church's inclusion of all members of Christ's body; it also refers qualitatively to the pattern of faith and practice that distinguishes orthodox Christianity from heresy and schism.

Consensus with remaining differences—Language employed by the Lutheran-Roman Catholic *Joint Declaration on the Doctrine of Justification* to describe the manner in which both communions arrived at an essential doctrinal agreement on the meaning of this doctrine, while allowing that there remained differences in the way each communion explicated the doctrine that were not insignificant but nevertheless not church-dividing. See also **differentiated consensus*.

Convergence—The movement of divided churches toward one another in *faith and order, mission, and service.

Dialogue of love—Rooted in the biblical teaching that "speaking the truth in love" (Eph 4:15) contributes to the unity of the church, it is a principle of Roman Catholic ecumenism that the starting place for ecumenical engagement is the recognition of separated Christians as brothers and sisters in Christ, which carries with it the obligation of being in dialogue with them and seeking to remove any obstacles to dialogue that have resulted from sinful hostility between separated Christians. See also **dialogue of truth*.

Dialogue of truth—A principle of Roman Catholic ecumenism also rooted in the biblical teaching that "speaking the truth in love" (Eph 4:15) contributes to the unity of the church, which requires that the recognition of separated brothers and sisters as fellow Christians in a *"dialogue of love" must proceed to an earnest discussion of significant differences with the goal of arriving at a unity in the truth.

Differentiated consensus—A term now commonly used to describe the sort of agreement reached between the Lutheran World Federation and the Roman Catholic Church in their *Joint Declaration on the Doctrine of Justification* (1999). While the Joint Declaration itself does not use the precise expression "differentiated consensus," the concept is certainly present in its language "consensus on basic truths" with "remaining differences" or "differing explications." It thus does not suggest complete doctrinal agreement, but an agreement substantial enough that the remaining differences are no longer regarded as church-dividing. The language "differentiated consensus" has become identified with the Joint Declaration in the process of its *reception. See also *consensus with remaining differences.*

Ecumenism—The quest for the *visible unity of the currently divided church.

Eucharistic sharing—One dimension of the *visible unity of the church, which is realized between particular communions when each recognizes the validity of the other's Eucharistic celebrations and when members of each communion are welcomed to receive the Eucharist in worship services of churches belonging to one another's denominational communions.

Exchange of gifts—see *Receptive ecumenism.*

Faith and Order—One of the three major interrelated streams of the modern ecumenical movement, Faith and Order involves candid theological dialogue about the issues of doctrine (the teachings of a church) and church order (a church's patterns of ordained ministry, governance, and baptismal and Eucharistic theology and practice) that presently prevent full *visible unity among the churches. The international institutional expression of Faith and Order ecumenism began with the World Council on Faith and Order in Lausanne, Switzerland, in 1927 and in 1948 joined with the *Life and Work movement to form the World Council of Churches.

Fundamental consensus—The attainment of a basic agreement on some matter of doctrine that previously divided the parties to an *interconfessional dialogue, an agreement that may nevertheless allow for significant remaining differences of explaining that doctrine that do not rise to the level of church-dividing differences. This is one component of a *"differentiated consensus."

Hierarchy of truths—The recognition by the Vatican II Decree on Ecumenism *Unitatis Redintegratio* that while there are some essential doctrines that cannot be compromised in efforts toward ecumenical *convergence, there are other doctrines that can admit expression through differing theological formulations that are not necessarily church-dividing; indeed they may be *"mutually complementary rather than conflicting." In context, the latter concession had in mind ecumenical relations between the Roman Catholic Church and the Eastern Orthodox Churches.

Interconfessional dialogue—Ecumenical dialogue between representatives of separated church/denominational communions. This is the larger category that includes both *bilateral dialogues and *multilateral dialogues.

Interreligious dialogue—Dialogue between representatives of the Christian churches and representatives of non-Christian religions, which has mutual understanding as its goal. While it is sometimes called a "wider ecumenism," it does not have as its aim the sort of visible unity that is the goal of *ecumenism proper, which is an intra-Christian rather than interreligious enterprise.

International Missionary Conference—One of the three major interrelated streams of the modern ecumenical movement, the quest for unity in the evangelistic mission of the church had its origins in the nineteenth-century modern mission movement, moved toward a more formal institutional expression with the World Missionary Conference in Edinburgh, Scotland, in 1910 and the formation of the International Missionary Conference in 1921, and in 1961 merged with the World Council of Churches that had been formed in 1948 with the merger of the *Faith and Order and *Life and Work movements.

Life and Work—One of the three major interrelated streams of the modern ecumenical movement that seeks to foster worldwide cooperation between the churches in addressing social issues, it had its official institutional beginning with the Conference on Life and Work in Stockholm, Sweden, in 1925. Though an early slogan of the movement was "doctrine divides, service unites," this stream of the ecumenical movement historically went hand-in-hand with a commitment to seeking greater unity in doctrine, and in 1948 it merged with the *Faith and Order movement to form the World Council of Churches.

Multilateral dialogue—Ecumenical dialogue between representatives of more than two church/denominational communions. Some multilateral dialogues are steps toward the formation of "uniting" churches of multiple denominational traditions; others lead to the drafting of texts intended to foster greater degrees of *convergence toward unity among the churches, such as the *Baptism, Eucharist and Ministry* document issued by the Faith and Order Commission of the World Council of Churches.

Mutual recognition—May refer to the recognition by two or more communions of one another's baptisms, Eucharistic celebrations, and/or orders of ministry as steps toward the attainment of *visible unity.

Mutually complementary rather than conflicting—With reference to the doctrinal formulations of churches, the recognition by the Vatican II Decree on Ecumenism *Unitatis Redintegratio* that in a *"hierarchy of truths" there are doctrines that can admit expression through differing theological formulations that are not necessarily church-dividing and indeed may serve to enrich one another and assist in expressing the doctrine more fully, even while there are also some doctrines that are essential and cannot be compromised. In context, the former concession had in mind ecumenical relations between the Roman Catholic Church and the Eastern Orthodox Churches.

New Delhi definition—The Third Assembly of the World Council of Churches in New Delhi, India, in 1961 adopted this definition of the goal of the ecumenical movement: "We believe that the unity which is both God's will and his gift to his Church is being made visible as all in each place who are baptized into Jesus Christ and confess him as Lord and Savior are brought by the Holy Spirit into one fully-committed fellowship, holding the one apostolic faith, preaching the one Gospel, breaking the one bread, joining in common prayer, and having a corporate life reaching out in witness and service to all and who at the same time are united with the whole Christian fellowship in all places and all ages, in such wise that ministry and members are accepted by all, and that all can act and speak together as occasion requires for the tasks to which God calls his people." This is now regarded by many as the definitive (and for the WCC, official) explanation of what it might mean for the churches to experience *visible unity.

Oikoumenē—A Greek word that originally referred to the whole inhabited world, *oikoumenē* came to be applied in Christian usage to the whole of the church spread throughout the world and thus supplied the root of the English terms "ecumenical" and *"ecumenism."

Reception—The process by which worldwide communions, national churches and denominations, local parishes and congregations, and individual Christians become informed about, consider, and act upon the proposals and agreements that result from bilateral and multilateral ecumenical dialogue.

Receptive ecumenism—An approach to ecumenical dialogue according to which the communions in conversation with one another seek to identify the distinctive gifts that each tradition has to offer the other and which each could receive from the other; given expression by Pope John Paul II in his 1995 encyclical on ecumenism *Ut Unum Sint* ("That

They May Be One"): "Dialogue is not simply an exchange of ideas. In some ways it is always an 'exchange of gifts'" (§ 28). Some *interconfessional dialogues, such as that between the Roman Catholic Church and the World Methodist Council, have worked toward concrete proposals for the exchange of ecclesial gifts.

Spiritual ecumenism—An approach to ecumenical engagement that begins with the already-present spiritual realities that unite all Christians, such as common allegiance to Christ as Lord, the indwelling of the Holy Spirit shared by all believers, and opportunities to pray together and share other experiences of worship even when Eucharistic fellowship and other expressions of full visible communion are not yet possible. Frequently called "the soul of the ecumenical movement," spiritual ecumenism supplies the motivation for participation in other expressions of the quest for Christian unity, aids and sustains such participation, and in and of itself contributes to convergence toward visible unity.

Thick ecumenism—An approach to ecumenical encounter that proceeds on the basis of a common commitment both to deep exploration of the ancient Christian tradition to which all denominational traditions today are heirs and to deep exploration of the particularities of the respective denominational traditions.

Thin ecumenism—An approach to ecumenical encounter that seeks to overcome difference through a too-easy identification of lowest common denominator agreements between traditions.

Unitatis Redintegratio—Approved on November 21, 1964 by the Second Vatican Council (*Vatican II), this Decree on Ecumenism (the Latin title of which translates as "The Repair of Unity") was the major twentieth-century turning point in the progress of the quest for Christian unity. It acknowledged that all churches, including the Roman Catholic Church, share responsibility for their contributions to the present divisions, explicitly affirmed that non-Catholic Christians experience the grace of God through the presence of Christ and the work of the Spirit in Christian communities that are outside the Roman Catholic Church, and irrevocably committed the Roman Catholic Church to participation in the various expressions of the modern ecumenical movement.

Unity in reconciled diversity—A category applied by the ecumenist Harding Meyer to the type of ecumenical *convergence represented by the Lutheran-Reformed "Leuenberg Agreement" of 1973, which led to a form of full communion between several European Lutheran and Reformed communions whereby their churches received one another's members to table fellowship and recognized the ordinations of one another's ministers while declaring other doctrinal differences to be expressions of "reconciled diversity." Some ecumenists hail this as a model for ecumenical advance, while others warn that agreements of this nature remove important incentives for contesting the remaining doctrinal differences en route to a unity in the truth.

Ut Unum Sint—A papal encyclical (the Latin title of which translates "That They May Be One") issued by Pope John Paul II on May 25, 1995 that reiterated the commitment of the Roman Catholic Church to ecumenical engagement that had been declared in the documents of the Second Vatican Council (*Vatican II), especially in the Decree on Ecumenism *Unitatis Redintegratio*, and in papal encyclicals of his predecessors. *Ut Unum Sint* is especially noteworthy for its invitation to non-Catholic Christians to join the pope in thinking together about ways in which the Petrine office (the office of the papacy) might be able to be of service to the whole church, Catholic and non-Catholic.

Vatican II—A shorthand reference for the Second Vatican Council, convened from 1962 to 1965, which is identified by the Roman Catholic Church as its twenty-first ecumenical council. Though often popularly portrayed as a council that liberalized Catholic teachings, the theological work that informed Vatican II depended on two interrelated and inseparable tasks: an "updating" of the way the Church connected the truth of divine revelation to the contemporary world, but only in light of a careful and critical "retrieval" of the biblical and historical sources of the Church's faith. Great care was taken to prepare and present the constitutions and decrees of Vatican II in such a way as to invite broad ecumenical appreciation, and the Decree on Ecumenism *Unitatis Redintegratio* officially committed the Roman Catholic Church to participation in the various expressions of the modern ecumenical movement.

Visible unity—The stated goal of the modern ecumenical movement, which seeks a unity that makes outwardly evident the spiritual unity that already unites all members of the body of Christ. A commonly accepted definition of visible unity is the *New Delhi definition adopted by the Third

Assembly of the World Council of Churches in New Delhi, India, in 1961, according to which visible unity entails that all baptized Christians in every place there are Christians fully belong to one another in a covenanted community that is both local and worldwide in which they share the historic faith of the church, are able to share in the celebration of the Eucharist together, jointly engage in mission and service, accept the ministers and members of one another's churches as their own, and speak prophetic words to the world with a unified voice when God calls them to do so.

Wider ecumenism—see *Interreligious dialogue*